T0295775

Specialised Tourism Products

Specialised Tourism Products: Development, Management and Practice

BY

NEVEN ŠERIĆ

University of Split, Croatia

IVANA KURSAN MILAKOVIĆ

University of Split, Croatia

AND

IVAN PERONJA

University of Split, Croatia

United Kingdom – North America – Japan – India – Malaysia – China

Emerald Publishing Limited
Emerald Publishing, Floor 5, Northspring, 21-23 Wellington Street, Leeds LS1 4DL

First edition 2024

British Library Cataloguing in Publication Data
A catalogue record for this book is available from the British Library

ISBN: 978-1-83549-409-7 (Print)
ISBN: 978-1-83549-408-0 (Online)
ISBN: 978-1-83549-410-3 (Epub)

INVESTOR IN PEOPLE

Neven: *To dear God who guides me and my children – Mia, Ela, Anea and Antoni.*
Ivana: *To my husband, Marko, who was and is my lighthouse.*
Ivan: *To my God and my family.*

Contents

List of Figures, Tables and Case Studies   *ix*

About the Authors   *xi*

Chapter 1   **Introductory Notes**   *1*

Chapter 2   **Development Process of a Specialised Tourism Product**   *25*

Chapter 3   **Development of Ideas and Concepts**   *47*

Chapter 4   **Developing and Shaping the Marketing Strategy**   *57*

Chapter 5   **Business Analysis and Marketing Test of a New
             Specialised Tourism Product**   *63*

Chapter 6   **Development of a Specialised Tourism Product and
             Market Testing**   *79*

Chapter 7   **Tourism Product Policy and Sales Policy**   *89*

Chapter 8   **Introduction of a Specialised Tourism Product on the
             Market**   *95*

Chapter 9   **Brand and Brand Management of the Specialised
             Tourism Product**   *103*

Chapter 10   **Development and Management of a Specialised
             Tourism Product:** *Stay at the Adriatic Lighthouses*   *123*

Chapter 11   **Final Conclusions**   *139*

References   *143*

List of Figures, Tables and Case Studies

Figures

Fig. 1.	Sequence of Stages in the Development Process of a New Specialised Tourism Product.	27
Fig. 2.	Perceptual Map in the Third Stage of the Development Process of a New Specialised Tourism Product.	35
Fig. 3.	Presentation of the BCG Matrix of Specialised Tourism Products of *Destination X*.	38
Fig. 4.	Stončica Lighthouse on the Island of Vis (Arrow).	82
Fig. 5.	The Sušac Lighthouse on the Island of the Same Name (in the Square).	83
Fig. 6.	A Recommended Model for Creating a Dark Tourist Product.	115

Tables

Table 1.	Researched Countries Classified Into Clusters.	15
Table 2.	Evaluation of the Overall Technical Efficacy of the Tourism Economy of the EU Member States.	16
Table 3.	Assessment of the Overall Technical Efficacy of the Tourism Economy of Non-EU Countries.	17
Table 4.	Assessment of Pure Technical Efficacy of Tourism Sectors of EU Member States.	18
Table 5.	Evaluation of the Pure Technical Efficacy of the Tourism Economy of Non-EU Countries.	19

Table 6.   An Example of the Weighted Index Method in
              Evaluating New Product Ideas.   52
Table 7.   Adventure Activities – Descriptive Data.   68

Case Studies

Case Study 1: Company X, Split, Croatia – *Split
Walking Tour*   28
Case Study 2: The Development Potential of Monastery
Tourism   29
Case Study 3: Company Y – Tourist Stay at the Lighthouse   30
Case Study 4: *Extreme Adriatic Warrior* – Extreme
Team Building   33
Comment on the Distribution of Tourism Products in
the BCG Matrix of Destination X   39
Case Study 5: Elaboration of Prototypes for the Tourist
Service, Stay in the Lighthouse   80
Case Study 6: *Dark Tourism*   111
Case Study 7: *Solo Female Travel*   116

About the Authors

Neven Šerić, PhD, is a Full Professor tenure at the Faculty of Economics Business and Tourism, University of Split, Croatia. He is still working in practice (consultant for creating and branding new tourist products). During 27 years of business career, he was the General Manager and a member of directors in some companies (Tehnicar; ACI, etc.). His known practice project is *Stone Lights* – touristic valorisation of Adriatic lighthouses. At the University, he is engaged in marketing courses (*Business logistics, Market research in tourism, Marketing strategy in tourism, Branding strategies* and *Marketing in hotel business*). Was an active participant in more than 100 scientific conferences (keynote speaker, member of the scientific boards...), published more than 100 articles in international scientific journals, and more than 200 professional articles. Neven is the author of 13 scientific books, 11 book chapters and 14 professional books. He serves as a member of the editorial board and reviewer of several journals. Member of Cromar, Anahei, chairmanship in some international association, member of the board in sport clubs, voluntary donor of blood (41 times). He got many rewards and acknowledgements (scientific books, confession *Blue Band* of Vjesnik – rescuing life on the sea, rector's award etc.). Neven is also an active English and French speaker and a passive Italian and German speaker. He is also a black belt karate master fourth Dan, Tae Kwon Do ITF master first Dan.

Ivana Kursan Milaković, PhD, is an Associate Professor at the Faculty of Economics, Business and Tourism, University of Split, Croatia. She has been working in practice for a decade in the IT sector in marketing job positions and is currently, for years, at the university within the marketing department. Here, she is engaged in several marketing courses, such as *Consumer behaviour, Marketing communication* and *Brand management*. Ivana is an active participant in many scientific conferences and has published in many international journals, such as the *International Journal of Advertising, Business Ethics, the Environment & Responsibility, Electronic Commerce Research and Applications, International Journal of Retail and Distribution Management, Journal of Fashion Marketing and Management* and *International Journal of Consumer Studies*. Ivana is a member of European Marketing Academy (EMAC) and Croatian Marketing Association (CROMAR). She serves as the editorial review board member of journals (e.g. *Journal of Current Issues and Research in Advertising*) and as an ad hoc reviewer for many scientific journals (e.g. *International Journal of Advertising, International Journal of Consumer Studies, Journal of Business Research, Journal of Retailing* *und Consumer Services, Journal of Fashion Marketing and Management*). Ivana is also an active English and German speaker and a passive Italian and Spanish speaker. She has won many prizes and acknowledgements throughout her work, such as the rector's award and awards for scientific papers, cooperation and visibility.

Ivan Peronja, PhD, is an Associate Professor at the Faculty of Maritime Studies, University of Split, Croatia. He has been working in the maritime industry, education and science for over 15 years. At the University of Split, Faculty of Maritime Studies, he held various positions, serving as the vice-dean for management and finance, program director for maritime management studies and head of the lifelong learning centre for professional studies at the University of Split. He conducts courses in *Maritime financial management, Economics for managers, Maritime and port management* and *Business process management*. He won the University of Split Science Award and has published over 60 scientific and professional papers. He actively participated in several scientific meetings in the country and abroad. Actively participating in numerous national and international scientific conferences, he has published a series of scientific articles in international journals such as the *Journal of Marine Science and Engineering, Cogent Engineering, Tourism, Our Sea, Transactions on Maritime Science* and *Scientific Journal of Maritime Research*. Additionally, he is a member of the organising and program committees for several domestic and international conferences. He is an ad hoc reviewer for domestic and international scientific and professional journals, such as the *Scientific Journal of Maritime Research* and *Transactions on Maritime Science*. He possesses practical knowledge and experience in corporate management, having held leading positions in supervisory and management boards in various companies and institutions.

Chapter 1

Introductory Notes

The trigger for this challenge was the first author's experience in developing and managing a new specialised tourism product – *lighthouse tourism*. That project [*Stone Lights – a stay at Adriatic lighthouses*] was developed during 1999–2001 and finally was introduced to the global tourism market (Šerić, 2004). Through experiences of creating and managing this project, the authors have acknowledged the specifics and legalities of implementing marketing for specialised tourism products. A few years after the commercialisation of the project and the positioning of the brand, *Stone Lights* conducted various scientific research related to practical experiences (Jakšić Stojanović et al., 2019a, 2019b; Jakšić Stojanović, Janković, Šerić, & Vukilić, 2019; Jakšić Stojanović, Šerić, et al., 2019; Šerić, 2014; Šerić & Luković, 2013; Šerić, Mihanović, et al., 2020). Presented reflections of the importance of specialised tourism products can also be found in the works of Butler (2020), Coasta (2020), Meler and Magaš (2014), and Angelevska Najdeska and Rakicevik (2012). All these findings are today linked to the pursuit of sustainable tourism development in the design of new specialised tourism products (Meler & Ham, 2012; Meler & Horvat, 2018; Nunkoo et al., 2019; Ruhanen et al., 2019).

The contribution of specialised tourism content to the attractiveness and competitiveness of the destination offer is growing following the negative implications of climate change and the COVID-19 pandemic on the global tourism economy (Gossling et al., 2020; Hall et al., 2020; Morrison, 2013; Prideaux et al., 2020; UNWTO, 2020; Wen et al., 2021; WTTC, 2020; Zhang et al., 2021). Scholars (e.g. Jafari & Xiao, 2021; Jenkins, 2020; Pineda et al., 2004; Šimundić et al., 2016; Waeaver, 2006) point to the need for a systematic approach to tourism development and the development of specialised tourism content.

After developing several specialised tourism products and testing them in practice, the author with selected colleagues consolidated the final knowledge into a concrete model presented in this book. The purpose of the book is to show it to a broader scientific and professional public.

Specialised Tourism Products, 1–24
Copyright © 2024 Neven Šerić, Ivana Kursan Milaković and Ivan Peronja
Published under exclusive licence by Emerald Publishing Limited
doi:10.1108/978-1-83549-408-020241001

1.1. Specialised Tourism Product

A specialised tourism product as a formal and scientific construct implies atypical and unusual tourist content and offers adapted to tourist segments that express interest in them (Jafari & Xiao, 2021; Kotler et al., 2009; Meler & Ham, 2012; Meler & Horvat, 2018; Šerić, Jakšić Stojanović, et al., 2023; Šerić & Perišić, 2012). Specialised tourism products are often based on complex content and need a complex marketing scenario and specific destination resources (Botti et al., 2009; Buhalis, 2000; Buhalis & Foerste, 2015; Doyle, 2002; Jakšić Stojanović et al., 2020). Creativity in defining the promotional features of a specialised tourism product contributes to its transformation into a tourist attraction (Jafari & Xiao, 2021; Jakšić Stojanović & Šerić, 2018). Such an offer should combine the totality of the tourist experience with the satisfaction of specific needs – adventure, health, gastronomic, culture and others (Richards, 2019). Depending on the resources on which each specialised tourism product is based, its content is specific. A more complex specialised tourism product enables more apparent differentiation and indirectly greater attractiveness (Jakšić Stojanović et al., 2019a). More significant differentiation and originality of a specialised tourism product is a prerequisite for a higher price (Botti et al., 2009; Buhalis, 2000; Ritchie & Crouch, 2003; Šerić, 2014; Šerić, Kalinić, et al., 2011).

A specialised tourism product consists of the following components (Šerić, 2018):

- Core content is the idea and context on which the marketing story is developed. The basic content ensures recognition and attracts tourists (in *lighthouse tourism* it is the experience of the life of lighthouse keepers in past – in isolation – Šerić, 2004).
- Expected content includes the features of the offer based on the perception of the promotion of a specialised tourism product to the target tourist clientele (in the *lighthouse tourism* it is accommodation in an object of cultural heritage located on the protruding capes of the island or cliffs in a preserved landscape).
- Additional content contributes to the continuous maintenance of the attractiveness of a specialised tourism product and enables modifications during its life cycle to maintain demand (in *lighthouse tourism* it includes all potential additional services/activities that could be offered to tourists during their stay – a joint fishing trip with the lighthouse keepers; education in preparing fish meals; kayaking, etc.).
- Expanded content contributes to the attractiveness of the specialised tourism product to the broader tourist population. If sales are unsatisfactory, this content is emphasised via promotion activities (in *lighthouse tourism* it could be guided diving courses, free climbing courses, fishing equipment and boat rental, organised gastronomic events and more). The expanded content of the specialised tourism product is developed by adapting it to tourism segments that do not show interest in the basic content of the offer.

Specialised tourism products have their life cycle (Jobber, 2001). To prolong the maturity phase, additional and expanded content is important. When refining the basic offer with additional and expanded content, one should take into account the profitability and preservation of the recognition of the basic content, primarily if the brand of a specialised tourism product is based on it (Barros & Alves, 2004; Kotler & Armstrong, 2001; Kušen, 2002). Regardless of the originality of the idea of a future specialised tourism product, the possibilities of developing additional and expanded content should also be considered. In the phase of introducing it to the market, the expected content of the specialised tourism product is critical. The perception of the expected content of potentially interested tourists indirectly contributes to matching the offer with their expectations (Buhalis & Foerste, 2015). The authors' and other practices have proven that with the growth of satisfied and loyal tourists, the influence of expected content on new client decreases (Kosmaczewska, 2014; Šerić, Jakšić Stojanović, et al., 2023; Šerić & Talijančić, 2011). The authors got the impression that tourists' perceptions of a specialised tourism product can be changed by changing the relationship between basic, additional and extended content (Jakšić Stojanović et al., 2020; Jakšić Stojanović & Šerić, 2018; Šerić, 2017, 2019b; Šerić, Jerković, et al., 2017; Šerić & Luković, 2013).

A specialised tourism product for which the demand continuously grows after its introduction can achieve significant commercial effects as a recognisable component of an integrated destination product (Šerić & Marušić, 2019; Šerić, Mihanović, et al., 2020). Therefore, the specialised tourism offer should be positioned according to the location's geographical and climatic specificities (Barros et al., 2011; Boes et al., 2016; Jafari & Xiao, 2021). To realise the synergistic effects of a specialised tourism offer with an integrated destination product, mutual harmony in identity and image is essential (Boes et al., 2016; Šerić et al., 2011). For this reason, the idea of a new specialised tourism product should also be considered geographically, related to a tourism destination whose offer the new content can easily fit into (Becken, 2005; Beeton, 2006; Cracolici et al., 2008).

Destination's tourism stakeholders are interested in developing new specialised content, as they are the basis for selective tourism forms (Cooper, 2021). A selective tourism offer is a prerequisite for a year-round tourist visit (Jafari & Xiao, 2021). By introducing new specialised content into the destination offer, visitors are indirectly encouraged to extend their stay (Jakšić Stojanović & Šerić, 2019a). The differentiation and originality of specialised tourism products make them practical for branding, and the striking impression of their brands contributes to strengthening the visibility of their destination (Buhalis & Sinarta, 2019; Morrison, 2013). The evolution of tourism as a specific social phenomenon encourages the development of specialised tourism products (Buhalis & Park, 2021; Buhalis & Sinarta, 2019). Economic development and technological changes contribute to this (Bi et al., 2011; Prorok et al., 2019). Capital encourages new investments, especially where it is possible to ensure a higher rate of returns (Bilandžić, 2008). Given that many specialised tourism products offer premium prices, it is always possible to interest potential investors in such investments (Barros et al., 2011; Boyer et al., 2011; Drucker, 1994; Fletcher, 2003; Šerić, Jakšić Stojanović, et al., 2023).

The global market of specialised tourism products is dynamic nowadays. Such offers are developing with the growth of tourist trips (Dolnicar, 2019). The internet and the intensive informatisation of society enable the rapid exchange of data and information, resulting in the development of new ideas for tourist content and offer (Borges et al., 2009; Chaffey et al., 2003; Jerkić & Šerić, 2014; Sheth et al., 2001). In the structure of the global tourism offers, specialised tourism products show a high growth rate during the last two decades and have increasingly significant implications for the growth of national tourism economies (Barros et al., 2011; Hadad et al., 2012; Prorok et al., 2019). Thus, specialised tourism products today represent one of the most dynamic and fastest growing categories of tourism. In contrast to seasonal tourism products, specialised tourism products are characterised by intensive growth and encouraging tourists to travel throughout the year. Specialised tourism products are also catalysts for faster tourism growth and the extension of the tourism season (Buhalis & Park, 2021). Specialised tourism products thus become the basis of the competitiveness of the national offer and a critical development factor of the tourism economy (Buhalis & Sinarta, 2019). Tourism stakeholders face a series of challenges and dilemmas in developing specialised tourism. This indicates the need for a more complex elaboration of proposals and ideas (Šerić & Jurišić, 2014; Šerić & Luković, 2010). Dealing with creating, developing, and commercialising specialised tourism products requires awareness of a systematic approach. It is the only way that contributes to the market success of the specialised tourism offer (Šerić, 2014). Managing the development of specialised tourism products implies the cooperation of destination stakeholders with partners in the sales chain (Phillips & Louvieris, 2005; Prorok et al., 2019; Šerić, 2018).

In addition to economic and social perspectives, developing new specialised tourism products also contributes to the growth of international openness and more intensive geographical connection and cross-border cooperation (Šerić et al., 2012). This impacts the continuity of population income growth and infrastructure development, indirectly contributing to a higher quality of life (Cooper, 2021; Jafari & Xiao, 2021; UN, 2020; Zhang et al., 2021). Managing the development of specialised tourism products implies specialist knowledge and a multidisciplinary approach (Buhalis & Sinarta, 2019). The good practice of managing specialised tourism products could be used to remove institutional and financial barriers in the commercialisation of valuable national resources (Šerić & Talijančić, 2011). Institutional obstacles to tourism commercialising valuable resources are particularly pronounced in post-transition countries. Representatives of local authorities are often not familiar with the possibilities of contributing specialised offers to the local tourism economy. The tourism economy represents a sustainable long-term development concept in all countries with resources for specialised tourism products (Jenkins, 2020; Prorok et al., 2019). Recent research on the consequences of the COVID-19 pandemic on the tourism economy indicates that specialised tourism products are more resilient than seasonal tourism products (Girish, 2020; Hall et al., 2020). Seasonal tourism products, unlike specialised ones, are more sensitive to all economic and social disturbances (Barros et al., 2011; Šerić & Meža, 2014).

The specialised tourism offer is a labour-intensive segment of the tourism economy because it often implies a year-round offer and engagement of various tourism specialists. The premium prices of such products are based on tourists' perception of added value (Buhalis & Foerste, 2015). Hired specialised tourism workers also contribute to the impression of added value. Thus, continuous development of specialised tourism products encourages self-employment, new jobs and positive implications for the growth given the local population's income in the receiving destination (Prorok et al., 2019). Many specialised tourism products are based on natural and cultural–historical resources (Jakšić Stojanović et al., 2019a; Šerić & Talijančić, 2011), which are largely well preserved in economically less developed countries.

Moreover, preserving these resources is an incentive for the continuity of developing new specialised tourism products. But tourism practice indicates that the creation of new specialised tourism products is often not standardised (Pivčević et al., 2016; Šimundić et al., 2016). Such an approach results in an uncontrolled intensity of valuable resource consumption and can make the specialised tourism offers in such countries unsustainable and unacceptable from a social point of view in the long term (Kušen, 2002; Meler & Magaš, 2014). This is why standardisation and a conceptual approach to developing specialised tourism products are essential. Developing specialised tourism products in post-transition tourist countries characterised by the seasonality of the visit has a positive influence on the extension of the tourism season (Prorok et al., 2019). However, conservation and diversity of resources are not enough. Namely, innovative ideas are needed (Jakšić Stojanović & Šerić, 2018; Meler & Škoro, 2013) and a systematic approach to the development of new specialised tourism products (Lehman & Winner, 2005; Šerić, 2020). In the area of Mediterranean countries, the growth of specialised tourism offers contributes to the balancing of regional economic development (Prorok et al., 2019).

In the global tourist market, the demand for specialised tourism products is growing (Šerić & Jurišić, 2015). From this perspective, it can be noted that there are significant opportunities to increase tourism income from specialised tourism products. This is especially important for countries with preserved resources for which the interest of tourists is growing (Prorok et al., 2019). With relatively modest investments in this offer segment, it is possible to achieve significant financial effects on the entire tourism economy. Despite the possibilities, preserved resources and existing infrastructure, many Mediterranean countries only earn a modest off-season tourism income (Prorok et al., 2019). This results from the slow transformation of existing resources into new specialised tourism facilities. The cause of the inefficient commercialisation of national resources is an unsystematic approach and a lack of tourism workers educated for developing specialised tourism products. Although the marketing practice of developing, promoting and selling specialised tourism products has begun to be researched in recent years, the modest literature is a problem in the education of tourism staff and practice.

The development and management of specialised tourism products have attracted the public's and scientists' attention in recent years (Buhalis & Foerste,

2015; Richards, 2019; Šerić, Jakšić Stojanović, et al., 2023). The requirements for tourism demand are changing rapidly, especially following the consequences of the COVID-19 pandemic (Gossling et al., 2020). The global recession and the growth of competition in tourism impose the need for changes in the management of national tourism offers (Prideaux et al., 2020). Large emission tourism markets have the most significant potential for the economic recovery of countries strategically oriented towards tourism. Changes in the perception and behaviour of tourists are also evident in these tourist markets (Wen et al., 2021; Zhang et al., 2021).

The specialised tourism offer is based on original and innovative content that often implies commercialising valuable natural, cultural, historical and other national resources. The sustainability of the specialised tourism offer is based on responsible spending and management of the valorisation of these resources (Ruhanen et al., 2019). These facts argue the need for a systematic approach to developing and managing specialised tourism products. The literature on this subject is very modest because people engaged in developing and managing specialised tourism content rarely publish their experiences. Recent tourism practice indicates that the target tourism segments do not recognise certain specialised tourism products. The promotion of these contents is often inappropriate, many are not branded or their brands are not managed effectively (Šerić, 2011, 2014; Šerić & Meža, 2014; Šerić & Perišić, 2012). In addition, the activities of marketing management of such content are ignored. Thus, many of the new specialised tourism products, after several years of commercialisation, end up in the graveyard zone of the receptive tourism offer (Šerić, Jakšić Stojanović, et al., 2023), which is similar to what happens with a brand if it is not systematically managed (Kotler et al., 2009).

The first author of the book was the leader of several projects for the development of specialised tourism products (Šerić, 2004, 2008, 2017; Šerić & Luković, 2010, 2013; Šerić & Perišić, 2012). In particular, lighthouse tourism is globally positioned as one of such projects (Šerić, 2004). This specialised tourism product was also featured on the cover page of Yahoo on the 12th July, 2005, with the headline 'Croatia's lighthouses lure adventure seekers'. After the commercialisation of the Stone Lights project, he and his collaborators have continued new projects for the development of specialised tourism products in neighbouring countries as well (Jakšić Stojanović et al., 2020; Jakšić Stojanović & Šerić, 2018). Existing experiences are continuously tested in business practice (Jakšić Stojanović et al., 2019a, 2019b; Šerić, 2018; Šerić, Jakšić Stojanović, et al., 2023; Šerić & Perišić, 2012).

1.2. Tourism Practice

The idea of a new specialised tourism product should be focused on potential new tourist needs (Jakšić Stojanović & Šerić, 2018; Šerić & Jurišić, 2015; Šerić & Marušić, 2019). In practice, a mistake is often made at the idea development stage by focusing on one exclusive resource that is considered to be commercialised with another contents. The focus is primarily on the resource instead of the final content of the offer. A resource that is a prerequisite for developing a specialised tourism offer is the platform, but it must not be a limitation of the whole idea (Lehman & Winner, 2005). Each destination resource can be valorised through several specialised tourism products. The attractiveness of a particular specialised tourism product will depend on its differentiation (adapted from Solow, 2008). So the focus should be on the originality of the new tourist content, not on the resource on which it is based. A diversified approach to tourist content based on the same destination resource is a prerequisite for implementing sustainable tourism standards (Peypoch, 2007). Concerning the sensitivity to commercialisation and the non-renewability of some resources, an unsystematic approach can result in degradation, i.e. a decrease in their value (Šerić & Luković, 2010; Šerić & Perišić, 2012). The findings of several studies have proven that in many countries, this is not taken into account (Cuccia et al., 2013; Prorok et al., 2019; Šimundić et al., 2016). The result is a multitude of economically unsustainable tourist attractions that endanger non-renewable resources.

The existing global offer of specialised tourism products stimulates new tourist needs, so this issue should be viewed in a broader context. Tourism opting for specialised content is a valuable source of new ideas. And this fact imposes a systematic approach to developing specialised tourism products. Systematic management of the valorisation of valuable destination resources, which are a prerequisite for an attractive and competitive specialised tourism product, guarantees their preservation. Despite their content and originality, many specialised tourism products do not achieve significant sales. Their life cycle is short; they are quickly introduced on the market and promptly withdrawn from the offer (Šerić, Peronja, et al., 2020). A small part of the specialised tourism offer manages to be maintained in the long term and thus contributes to the competitiveness of the particular destination.

A systematic approach to developing and managing a specialised tourism product presupposes a scientific foundation and argumentation based on examples of good practice with rational use of the destination's resources. Ideas for potential new specialised tourism products should be sought between the existing destination offer and loyal visitors' desires. In practice, ideas for new tourism content are generated exclusively according to the current logistics infrastructure. Destination possibilities and available resources are an assumption, but they should not be a limitation for the ideas of new specialised tourism products. The flexibility of thinking and the willingness to modify existing ideas of new content prolongs the process of developing a new tourism offer but enables valuable knowledge about the necessary characteristics.

A specialised tourism product that has reached maturity is often characterised by routine provision/service and a price acceptable to tourists. Such a market-successful specialised tourism product results from a clear idea of future content that targets certain segments of the tourism population. As a result, the specialised tourism offer should be positioned in a market niche where it will be visible, thus ensuring a satisfactory return on investment. When monitoring global tourism trends, it is worth determining the order in which tourists choose unique tourist destinations, accommodation entities and specialised tourism facilities. Facts are often not what they seem (UNWTO, 2020). Deviations in tourists' reactions and purchasing decisions from what was expected in the post-COVID era are even more challenging to understand (WTTC, 2020). For this reason, much more time should be devoted to developing and planning the future specialised tourism product than 20 or more years ago. A creative and attractive specialised tourism product is not based solely on the genius of the idea but also on the appreciation of relevant market facts, rational thinking and the connection of stakeholders that will ensure the necessary quality through synergy. Focusing on a narrower tourism segment does not stimulate mass demand. Still, it allows the content to be adjusted to the expectations of the target population, which is a prerequisite for a higher price. Such a specialised offer's long-term sustainability and profitability can be based on high quality and evident added value. In current tourism practice, especially in the post-transition Mediterranean countries, it is often about incomplete content that is sometimes characterised by a lower quality of service. This is often the result of an unsystematic approach to developing and commercialising specialised tourism products.

1.3. Specialised Tourism Products as Tourism Growth Catalysts

Specialised tourism offer is an essential competitive component of every national tourism offer (Prorok et al., 2019). Such facilities stimulate the growth of tourist visits and draw the attention of the global tourism public to a receptive tourism country (Buhalis, 2000). A systematic approach to developing and managing a specialised tourism offer significantly impacts the economy of receptive countries with a relevant tourism share regarding the gross national product (Cvetkoska & Barišić, 2014). This is especially important for small post-transition countries with the prospect of tourism growth (Prorok et al., 2019). Such countries should use special policies and measures to support and stimulate the development of specialised tourism products.

1.3.1. Argumentation

Today, the tourism economy in Europe represents one of the most dynamic and fastest growing activities (Toma, 2014; UN, 2020). During the last two decades, it has been characterised by continuous growth (Cooper, 2021). In many post-transition countries, tourism is an important catalyst for developing the national economy (Prorok et al., 2019). This indicates the need to face the challenges imposed by global tourism trends. Concerning the growing interest of the tourism public in specialised tourism products, this issue needs to be systematically regulated by national policies (Jafari & Xiao, 2021). The positive economic and social implications of the tourism economy on a receptive tourism country are part of the possible repercussions on the living standards of the local population (Beeton, 2006). Developing specialised tourism content results in greater international openness of the country, cross-border cooperation and interesting economic connection with neighbouring countries (Šerić et al., 2012). The income of residents employed in tourism is growing, and the transport infrastructure is also improving (Šimundić et al., 2016).

The contribution of tourism income to the growth of GDP, living standards and the financial solvency of the country stimulate national support for the specialised tourism offer. Such tourist offer is resistant towards many internal and external market disturbances (Buhalis et al., 2019). Specialised tourism products are labour-intensive if they imply additional knowledge and experience for guiding and animating tourist groups. A specialised tourist offer rarely means cheaper labour. Tourist employees who provide such services should be adequately educated and have the necessary experience. Many specialised tourism products are based on natural and cultural–historical resources (Šerić & Talijančić, 2011). Systematic management of the development of a specialised tourism offer contributes to balancing the national tourism income in the long term (Šerić & Perišić, 2012). From the aspect of maintaining global tourism demand, specialised tourism offers' perspectives and growth potentials are particularly important for the economy of small post-transition countries (Prorok et al., 2019). It contributes to the global visibility of less developed countries with relevant and preserved resources.

In accordance with current tourism global trends, national measures to encourage the development of selective forms of tourism (e.g. health tourism, dark tourism, cultural tourism, creative tourism, adventure, sports and educational tourism) are also a prerequisite for the sustainability of the national tourism economy (Buhalis & Sinarta, 2019). However, when adopting support policies and strategic development guidelines at the national level and the level of destinations, it is necessary to consider the responsible and sustainable valorisation of the resources needed for developing specialised tourism offers (Cantino et al., 2018).

1.3.2. Recent Studies' Results

Recent research on tourism phenomena is often focused on evaluating the tourism efficiency of regions, countries and groups of countries to define the tourism development strategy. For example, in the case of France, Peypoch (2007) analysed the results of applying the Luenberger productivity indicator and the Malmquist index in evaluating the efficiency of the tourism sector in the period from 2000 to 2003. The analysis confirmed the advantage of the Luenberger indicator compared to the Malmquist productivity index (it overestimates changes in productivity and implies input or output orientation, which results in the decomposition of total tourism productivity into efficiency changes and technological development). The influence of the specialised tourism offer is significant in this regard. This was followed by research by Botti et al. (2009). They analysed the efficiency of 22 tourism regions in France using the output-oriented Data Envelopment Analysis (DEA) method. The analysis is based on the number of tourists as an output variable and on six input variables (number of hotels, campsites, parks, monuments, museums and size of beaches). They demonstrated technical efficiency in 10 regions characterised by a specialised tourism offer. A similar analysis of the tourism efficiency of 22 tourist regions in France was conducted by Barros et al. (2011) for the period from 2003 to 2007 using the two-stage DEA method. In the first phase, they evaluated efficiency coefficients for each tourist region based on two input variables (number of accommodation capacities and number of tourist arrivals) and one output variable (number of overnight stays). In the second phase, by applying regression analysis and including the variable of tourism attractions (monuments, museums, parks, beaches, ski resorts and nature parks), they realised that the content of the offer and the location where something is offered contribute significantly to the effectiveness of the tourism product. Their findings proposed new specialised tourism products based on theme parks, monumental heritage, winter tourism resources and nature parks, arguing the potential of developing specialised tourism products for the national economy. The findings of this research call for the need to transition from mass tourism to tourism with specialised products adapted to the specific needs of tourists. Cracolici et al. (2008) analysed the technical efficiency of tourism destinations in 103 Italian regions during 2001. Competitiveness in terms of technical efficiency was examined using the parametric Stochastic Frontiers Analysis (SFA) method and the non-parametric DEA method. The findings obtained by the SFA method proved that the variability of the efficiency index among the observed regions is affected by the development of specialised tourism content. In addition, areas with historical and cultural tourism content achieve higher tourist efficiency indices than the regions where mass tourism prevails. Somewhat lower efficiency ratings were obtained using the DEA method, which was interpreted as insufficient homogeneity of the regions included in the research sample. Using the two-stage DEA method, Cuccia et al. (2013) proved the impact of UNESCO nominations on the efficiency of tourist destinations and tourist travel routes in the regions of Italy for the period from 1995 to 2010. The findings of these studies also proved the influence of specialised tourism content on the development of the tourism economy. Furthermore, the results of all the studies mentioned above argue that the available resources are insufficient for the growth of the tourist economy. Specialised tourism offer based on these resources contribute significantly to the growth of the tourist economy and GDP.

The development of a specialised tourism offer economically multiplies the value of national resources, and the sustainability of tourism growth at the national level is questionable without specialised tourism products. National resources under UNESCO protection do not significantly impact the efficiency of the national tourism economy if not commercialised by various forms of selective tourism. These findings are an incentive for analysing the efficiency of the tourism economy of less developed European countries. A long-term sustainable tourism development strategy in these countries can have significant positive implications for their national economy. This strategy should prioritise valorising and commercialising valuable national resources by offering innovative and attractive specialised tourism products. One study for these purposes is Toma (2014) – analysed eight regions in Romania in 2012 using the input-oriented DEA method. The analysis proved the effectiveness of five regions. In ineffective regions, the lack of specialised tourist facilities is evident. They evaluated the efficiency of 31 provinces in the capacity-building stage and the benefit-creating stage. In the first phase, 19 provinces proved to be tourism efficient, and in the second, 22 of them. According to the overall evaluation, only six provinces showed an efficiency coefficient equal to one, while the worst-rated province had an efficiency coefficient of 0.3890. The research findings argue the pointlessness of basing the tourism economy solely on receptive capacities and the accompanying logistics infrastructure if the development of specialised tourism content is neglected.

Cvetkoska and Barišić (2014) measured the efficiency of the tourism economy of 15 European countries (i.e. Austria, Bosnia and Herzegovina, Bulgaria, Croatia, Cyprus, the Czech Republic, France, Greece, Italy, Macedonia, Montenegro, Portugal, Serbia, Slovenia and Spain) from 2004 to 2013 using the DEA method and window analysis technique. By selecting two input and two output variables, with the formation of six periods within every 5 years, the highest efficiency ratings were reported in 2004, while the lowest ones were achieved in 2011. The obtained results proved that no single country included in the research achieved total efficiency in the analysed years. The share of specialised tourism content in the national tourism offer was assessed as modest. Ten out of 15 countries reported an efficiency coefficient greater than 0.95. Montenegro was identified as the country with the lowest efficiency in the tourism economy, while Italy, Cyprus, France and Spain achieved the highest ratings. In the tourist offers of those countries, a significant share of specialised tourism content is evident. In her research, Kosmaczewska (2014) covered 27 members of the European Union in the period from 2007 to 2009. The research findings proved that countries with higher GDP achieved a higher degree of technical efficiency in the tourism economy, while post-transition developing countries achieved a higher degree of volume efficiency. This can be explained by the fact that tourism development is determined significantly by the number of investments, which are more significant in more economically developed countries. However, the further growth of the efficiency of the tourism economy in these countries will significantly depend on the available resources for developing new specialised tourism products.

The authors claim that investments in the tourism economy of countries lacking resources for developing selective forms of tourism offers will decline. This represents an argument for encouraging sustainable tourism based on selective forms of offers (Milano et al., 2019). It is necessary to rank the available national resources that can be used to develop a specialised tourism offer and decide on specific categories of tourism products. Martín et al. (2015) developed a global competitiveness index and ranked 139 countries using the DEA method, considering their geographic location and current GDP. Concerning the differences in the characteristics of the best and worst rated countries, this research also proved the importance of selective forms of the tourism offer. They also contributed significantly to mapping profiles that can be used to define national policies in the function of the tourism development strategy in order to improve the competitiveness of the tourism economy by encouraging the development of new specialised tourism products.

1.3.3. Authors' Research Findings

The relevance of research findings on the efficiency of the tourism economy, which were reached by applying the DEA method in combination with other parametric and non-parametric methods, defined the methodological framework for the author's research. The same was done to rank European countries according to the efficiency of the tourism economy and the needs of national tourism development strategies. This is also relevant to the scientific argumentation of the recommended support for developing specialised tourism products.

The DEA method is a valuable starting point for decision-making in optimising the tourism economy at the national level and arguing the importance of specialised tourism offers (Hadad et al., 2012). Limitations, regarding the usage of a large number of output and input variables, were handled by introducing the input and output variables representing the basic components of creating and providing a tourism product. Such a limitation does not distort the DEA method's output results and the findings' precision increases. In modifying the DEA method, the authors eliminated the concept's weaknesses by arranging the analysed countries into relatively homogeneous categories according to the similarity of available tourism resources. The number of defined input and output variables is adapted to the number of units in the research sample. The critical input variables are determined based on the main components and 14 criteria used by the World Economic Forum (WEF) to measure the success of countries in travel and tourism. The criteria were divided into four categories:

(1) business environment;
(2) conditions of tourism business;
(3) infrastructure;
(4) resources.

On the basis of these categories, an index of travel and tourism competitiveness was formed, which measured the efficiency of the national tourism economy. Given that countries and tourism regions differ in terms of the level of tourism competitiveness achieved, it is evident that all factors do not have an equal impact on the tourism performance in the analysed countries. For this reason, the fundamental variables that contribute to the tourism competitiveness of European countries have been identified. The research divides the countries into two groups: European Union member countries (28 countries) and non-European Union countries (14 countries). Two main components were identified for both groups of countries. For the member states of the European Union, it was determined that all variables with the highest factor loading, which make up the first component, have a positive sign:

• business environment;
• human resources and labour market;
• technological development;
• international openness;

- sustainability of the level of environmental preservation;
- road and maritime infrastructure.

The second component consists of variables:

- national treatment of the tourism sector;
- price competitiveness;
- air transport infrastructure;
- tourist infrastructure;
- landscape resources;
- cultural and historical resources and intensity of business trips.

Concerning the mentioned variables, only price competitiveness has a negative factor value. The rest of the variables indicate positive factor values. These results suggest that if a country is rated positively as a tourism destination by at least one feature of the component that determines it, it will also be highly rated by other features with the same sign of that component. In addition, countries rated highly for some features with a positive sign are ranked worse for some features with a negative sign. Thus, the countries of the European Union that belong to the group whose tourism economy is determined by another component show worse price competitiveness ratings. This is especially the case if they are rated highly according to other variables related to tourism and air transport infrastructure, landscape, cultural and historical resources and the intensity of business trips. A similar structure of components is also found in countries that are not members of the European Union. The structure of the first component consists of variables:

- business environment;
- security;
- human resources and labour market;
- technological development;
- national treatment of the tourism sector;
- international openness;
- price competitiveness;
- sustainability of the level of environmental preservation;
- road and maritime infrastructure;
- tourist infrastructure.

Three variables are included in the structure of the second component:

(1) air transport infrastructure;
(2) landscape resources;
(3) cultural and historical resources and intensity of business trips.

The identified main components were used in the research as input variables in evaluating the efficiency of the tourism economy. For the argumentation of the grouping of European Union countries and non-European Union countries, a cluster analysis was conducted. Here, hierarchical cluster analysis and k-cluster analysis were used to determine the optimal number of clusters and assigned countries to defined clusters. Four groups of countries have been identified for European Union member countries, while three groups of countries have been identified for non-European Union countries. Based on Anova's analysis, it was confirmed that the clusters thus formed are statistically significant for both groups of countries. Table 1 presents the results of the cluster analysis, with the definition of positively and negatively profiled components for each cluster individually.

The development of the tourist economy significantly impacts economic and non-economic aspects of development. The economic functions of tourism are manifested by a direct impact on GDP, the growth of less developed areas, the balance of payments and employment and an indirect effect on the development of industry, construction and agriculture, as these sectors market their products and services on the receptive tourist market. The social aspects of the development of the tourist economy relate primarily to health care, cultural and entertainment activities, social affairs and politics. There is an evident feedback loop because health, culture, entertainment, and social and political functions as social functions have significant repercussions on tourism development. Neglecting the links with these social functions weakens the leverage of the tourism economy on the development of society. The overall and pure technical efficiency of the national tourism economies of European countries was assessed using the output- and input-oriented Co Creation Readlines (CCR) and Basic Carring Capacity (BCC) models. Two groups of countries were analysed, as in the first part of the research. For both groups of countries, two input and two output variables were determined to evaluate the efficiency of tourism economies. The input variables for both groups of countries were obtained based on the scores of 14 criteria defined in the annual report on the tourism competitiveness of countries for 2017 published by the WEF. The number of input variables was reduced by applying the principal components method. For both countries, the characteristics were formed according to two input components based on a linear combination of 14 defined criteria. Considering that the linear combinations for the groups of countries are different, the evaluations of the efficiency of their tourism economies were assessed separately. The structure of the selected main features has already been presented. Data on the total contribution of the tourism economy to GDP expressed in percentages, and data given the direct contribution of the tourism economy to the employment growth rate, expressed in percentages, were used as output variables. The data on the input variables referred to the year 2017 and were downloaded from the World Data Atlas website (https://knoema.com/atlas 09/12/2019). Tables 2 and 3 show the results of the assessment of the overall technical efficiency of the tourism economy of EU member states and non-EU member states using the input-oriented CCR model. Countries are ranked by the efficiency of the national tourism economy. The DEA-Solver-LV software package was used for analysis.

In terms of the overall technical efficacy of the tourist economy, Cyprus, Malta and Bulgaria received the highest ratings. The value of the efficacy coefficient for

Table 1. Researched Countries Classified Into Clusters.

	EU Members' Clusters					Non-EU Countries' Clusters		
	C1	**C2**	**C3**	**C4**		**C1**	**C2**	**C3**
	Austria, Germany, Great Britain, Ireland	France, Italy, Greece, Portugal, Spain, Cyprus, Malta, Croatia	Luxembourg, Netherlands, Denmark, Finland, Sweden	Belgium, Czech Republic, Estonia Hungary, Latvia, Lithuania, Poland, Slovakia, Slovenia, Bulgaria, Romania	⇕	Switzerland, Norway, Iceland	Turkey, Ukraine, Russia	Serbia, Bosnia and Herzegovina, Macedonia, Albania, Montenegro, Moldova, Georgia, Armenia
PC1	PC1	PC2 and PC1	PC2	Countries in which both defined components have a negative profile and do not contribute to their tourism competitiveness	Positively profiled components:	PC1 and PC2	PC2	Countries in which both defined components are negatively profiled and do not contribute to their tourism competitiveness
PC2	PC2	PC1	PC1		Negatively profiled components:		PC1	

Source: Authors' research (2019).

Table 2. Evaluation of the Overall Technical Efficacy of the Tourism Economy of the EU Member States.

Country (DMU)	Efficacy Grade	Range
Cyprus	1	1
Malta	1	1
Bulgaria	1	1
Portugal	0.9911	4
Croatia	0.9225	5
Greece	0.7269	6
Estonia	0.6906	7
Ireland	0.6901	8
Poland	0.6761	9
Sweden	0.6116	10
Spain	0.5804	11
Romania	0.5493	12
Slovenia	0.5336	13
Netherlands	0.507	14
Italy	0.4797	15
Latvia	0.4126	16
Czech Republic	0.389	17
Finland	0.3722	18
Hungary	0.3587	19
Denmark	0.3453	20
Slovakia	0.3421	21
Luxembourg	0.2756	22
Belgium	0.2511	23
Lithuania	0.2197	24
Austria	0	25
France	0	25
Germany	0	25
Great Britain	0	25

Source: Authors' research (2019).

the three mentioned countries is 1, which indicates that these countries have achieved total technical efficacy of the tourism economy and represent a reference according to which the relative efficacy of the tourism economies of other countries is determined. Portugal (0.9911) and Croatia (0.9225) achieved

Table 3. Assessment of the Overall Technical Efficacy of the Tourism
Economy of Non-EU Countries.

Country (DMU)	Efficacy Grade	Range
Turkey	1	1
Albania	1	1
Montenegro	1	1
Gruzija	1	1
Ukraine	1	1
Armenia	1	1
Moldova	0.8913	7
Macedonia	0.7826	8
Bosnia and Herzegovina	0.6115	9
Serbia	0.4268	10
Russia	0.3057	11
Iceland	0.004	12
Switzerland	0	13
Norway	0	13

Source: Authors' research (2019).

somewhat lower ratings for the efficacy of the tourist economy, followed by
Greece (0.7269), Estonia (0.6906), Ireland (0.6901) and others.

In the group of countries not members of the European Union, Turkey,
Albania, Montenegro, Georgia, Ukraine and Armenia showed the most pro-
ductive tourism economy with a coefficient of 1. Given the Balkan EU non-
members, which belong to cluster 3 regarding the defined input variables, the
highest ratings of the efficiency of the tourism economy were given by Albania
and Montenegro. At the same time, Macedonia, Bosnia and Herzegovina and
Serbia showed relatively poor ratings for the overall technical efficacy of the
tourism economy. It should be noted that the application of the output-oriented
CCR model would give identical evaluations about the efficacy of the tourist
economy, but the orientation would be different.

Tables 4 and 5 show the results of the evaluation of the pure technical efficacy
of the tourism economy for EU member states and non-EU member states. Pure
technical efficacy was measured by applying the input-oriented BCC model, using
the DEA-Solver-LV software package.

The assessment of pure technical efficacy for the European Union member
states proved that most countries achieve full efficacy. Nonetheless, France,
Austria, Germany and Great Britain still have space for improvement. The
coefficient of pure technical efficacy for these countries is equal to zero. However,
the coefficient of their overall technical efficacy is equal to zero, but they occupy

Table 4. Assessment of Pure Technical Efficacy of Tourism Sectors of EU Member States.

Country (DMU)	Efficacy Grade	Return to Volume	Range
Cyprus	1	Constant	1
Malta	1	Constant	1
Bulgaria	1	Constant	1
Portugal	1	Increasing	1
Croatia	1	Increasing	1
Greece	1	Increasing	1
Estonia	1	Increasing	1
Ireland	1	Increasing	1
Poland	1	Increasing	1
Sweden	1	Increasing	1
Spain	1	Increasing	1
Romania	1	Increasing	1
Slovenia	1	Increasing	1
Netherlands	1	Increasing	1
Italy	1	Increasing	1
Latvia	1	Increasing	1
Czech Republic	1	Increasing	1
Finland	1	Increasing	1
Hungary	1	Increasing	1
Demark	1	Increasing	1
Slovakia	1	Increasing	1
Luxembourg	1	Increasing	1
Belgium	1	Increasing	1
Lithuania	1	Increasing	1
France	0.0001	Increasing	25
Austria	0	Increasing	26
Germany	0	Increasing	26
Great Britain	0	Increasing	26

Source: Authors' research (2019).

high positions given tourism indicators (tourist income, number of tourists and overnight stays, number of employees in tourism). Hence, it is evident that tourism development is based on the efficacy of economies of scale. In the category of countries that are not members of the European Union, almost all achieve

Table 5. Evaluation of the Pure Technical Efficacy of the Tourism Economy of Non-EU Countries.

Country (DMU)	Efficacy Grade	Return to Volume	Range
Turkey	1	Constant	1
Albania	1	Constant	1
Montenegro	1	Constant	1
Georgia	1	Constant	1
Ukraine	1	Constant	1
Armenia	1	Constant	1
Moldova	1	Increasing	1
Macedonia	1	Increasing	1
Bosnia and Herzegovina	1	Increasing	1
Serbia	1	Increasing	1
Russia	1	Increasing	1
Iceland	0.9999	Decreasing	12
Switzerland	0.0001	Increasing	13
Norway	0	Increasing	14

Source: Authors' research (2019).

pure technical efficacy. Only Switzerland and Norway have an efficacy coefficient equal to zero. In addition, all Western Balkans countries have a coefficient of pure technical efficacy similar to unity. In addition to achieving pure technical efficacy, Albania and Montenegro also achieve volume efficacy due to their coefficient of total technical efficacy being equal to unity. Countries with a lower coefficient of total technical but high pure technical efficacy value do not achieve efficacy in volume. These are Macedonia, Bosnia and Herzegovina and Serbia. The lower value of the CCR coefficient and the high value of the BCC coefficient means that these countries' tourism economies are efficacious at the national level but not at the global level, which is a consequence of volume inefficacy. The volume inefficacy in tourism practice is a consequence of insufficiently efficacious operational activities and insufficiently regulated and stimulating conditions of tourism development at the national level.

The findings of the conducted research argue the necessity of an appropriate national policy for developing selective forms of tourist offer, i.e. for encouraging the development of specialised tourism products. The valorisation and commercialisation of tourism resources on which potential growth is based should be carried out systematically. National political elites should be aware of the significance and sensitivity of the tourism economy. It is recommended, at the level of each tourist country, to look at the existing tourism development strategy and to revise the national policies that treat the tourism economy and resource management on which the development of selective forms of tourism offer is based. Suppose specialised tourism products are not significantly represented within the national tourism product. In that case, this offer segment has the prospect of a significant impact on the growth of tourism income and the national economy as a whole. According to the coefficients, the countries that ended up in the lower part of the tables are characterised by a significant volume of tourist visits, which can threaten and reduce the value of the resources on which the development of specialised tourism products depends. And the long-term sustainability of the national tourist offer depends on this offer segment.

The research findings benefit countries that are not yet members of the European Union. None of the two components defined in the research contributes positively to overall tourism competitiveness (low ratings of overall technical efficacy and consequently low volume efficacy). This suggests the need for prompt adoption of new national policies that will define the direction of the tourism development strategy, as the existing approach needs to be changed. These countries' tourism development strategies should focus on improving the 14 criteria that comprise the tourism competitiveness index. Such a determination would contribute to the growth of the attractiveness of existing tourism content, initiatives for developing new, particularly specialised tourism products, and indirectly to the growth of investments in the tourism economy.

The harmony of tourism development strategies in cross-border areas contributes to the growth of attractiveness and competitiveness of the wider region, which can significantly impact the overall economic development of the region and each country individually (Edgell et al., 2008; Šerić et al., 2012). Such a development scenario would encourage faster accession of current non-members to the European Union. This indicates that selective forms of tourism, i.e. the development of specialised tourism products, have an essential role. Therefore, tourism workers must be educated in their systematic development, which was an important incentive for writing this book.

1.4. Marketing in the Development of Specialised Tourism Products

Marketing activities are a vital lever in developing and managing a specialised tourism product. The focus in implementing these activities should be on the target tourism population. Who is the client that could first be won over and made loyal to the new specialised tourism product? By answering that question, the guidelines for evaluating and elaborating the idea of a potential new specialised tourism product are being comprehended. In doing so, one should keep in mind specialised tourism products with similar content and those that offer the prospect the opportunity to create an adequate and competitive substitute offer. It is complex to develop a wholly original and innovative specialised tourism product nowadays (Buhalis & Park, 2021). It is important that the differentiation, in terms of design compared to existing similar tourism products, can be used in promotion. All features of a potential new specialised tourism product that contribute to the attractiveness of one compared to other tourism offers of the same content category must be implemented in concept (adapted from Best, 2010).

The fact that a specialised tourism product is new in the global market does not guarantee its acceptance by the target tourism segment. Moreover, it is also difficult to predict its lifespan. Sometimes, it is precise because of the assessed risks related to the possible lifespan of a potential specialised tourism product that the further development of a good idea is abandoned. Marketing plays an important role precisely in the analysis of the viability of the idea of a new specialised tourism product. Various practical tools presented in the book are used for this purpose.

The affection of the target tourism segment for the new specialised tourism product is being created gradually (Coasta, 2020). It is important for communication to be two-way, and establishing such communication between those who offer and tourists implies time. For this reason, during the process of developing a specialised tourism product, market tests and analyses of the attitudes of the target tourism clientele should be carried out continuously. At the same time, care should be taken to ensure that the future new tourism product is not overexposed to the scrutiny of potential competitors. Specialists should focus marketing communication on features that are assumed to significantly impact the creation of tourist loyalty towards the specific tourism offer. The impression of a specialised tourism product is expressed as a complex set of perceptions, images and feelings that differentiate it from the existing tourism offer. The tourists experience and interpret the specialised tourism product based on specific needs and expectations following the information at their disposal.

The decision to develop a specific tourism offer depends on the assessment of attractiveness in the perception of target tourists. Their perception will depend on the impression of the quality and originality of the promotion (Sheehan et al., 2010). The growth of specialised tourism offers in the global tourism market also results in changes in the interests of tourists (Šerić & Meža, 2014). Acknowledging this fact, it is advisable to define standards that contribute to the clarity of what is offered to tourists during the development of the idea and concept of a specialised tourism product. The defined standards are a helpful starting point for thinking about ideas for future specialised tourism products.

Given that the diversity of secondary and tertiary characteristics of the specialised tourist offer is sufficient to attract the attention of a certain market segments, marketing analysis of possible different perceptions of the content will also be useful. It is essential to recognise the features that can be used to argue the potential added value of a specialised tourism offer in marketing communication (positive effects on human health, strengthening of immunity, socialisation, new acquaintances and the like). Neglecting to communicate the specific differences of a new specialised tourism product, compared to the promotion of similar offers, can result in reduced market visibility. The same happens when it is positioned in a market niche that does not allow it the necessary level of differentiation (the key features of a specialised tourism product are not of interest to tourists who choose offers from that niche). These are the causes that make the new tourism content, despite its innovation, insufficiently noticeable on the market. The consequences are slow demand growth and modest incomes during the first years of commer-cialisation, which sometimes results in the withdrawal of the specialised tourism product from the market.

Suppose the target tourist population reacts affirmatively to the new offer (they ask for additional information, frequent inquiries about free dates, etc.). In that case, it is practical to use the established connection with the tourism public further to adapt the characteristics to the target tourism segment. Modifications of the final concept of a specialised tourism product, sometimes minimal, can represent an additional incentive for the first purchase, contributing to the growth of demand due to passing on tourists' experiences.

Marketing research while developing a new specialised tourism product will answer relevant questions and dilemmas about the reality of target emitting tourism markets. Based on these findings, it is possible to predict the future of the specialised tourism product and the necessary modifications to maintain demand. Tourism is a specific social phenomenon, so marketing activities are imperative to maintain interest in demand. Tourists look primarily at the characteristics that are particularly attractive to them, especially in a specialised tourism product. The perception of the same tourism offer by different tourist segments can be different. Each tourist experiences the specialised tourism offer differently (Baker, 2007). The intensity of the attraction depends on its exposure to the promotion (adapted from Aaker et al., 1992). Which specialised tourism offer will attract the most attention of an individual tourist depends on the interest in the categories of tourism content offered, previous experiences, expectations and fears and whether the service quality will correspond to the promised (Cooper, 2021).

Tourists opt for specialised offers that stimulate attractive associations (good service and pleasant service staff, new experiences and new experiences) and are aligned with their needs and desires. When choosing a new specialised tourism product, i.e. making a tentative purchase decision, it is useful to determine the basic features that attract the tourists (Šerić & Ljubica, 2018). For one tourism segment, the variety of content is more important; for another, the price; for the third, the period of the year when something is offered. If a new tourism product targets a specific tourist segment, it is necessary to evaluate the ethical accept-ability of the same from the aspect of a particular social group (Beeton, 2006).

The practice has proven to the authors that the reaction of tourists to a new specialised tourism product also depends on links between the content and the personality of the targeted individual tourist (Šerić, 2004). Similar specialised tourism products are chosen given similar psychological profiles of tourists, so preliminary research during the process of developing new content can provide helpful information for the final version of the offer. In recent years, neuro-marketing research has also been practised for the sake of psychoanalytic and socio-psychological knowledge about personality traits (Šerić, Ljubica, et al., 2015). Psychoanalytic theory starts from the fact that tourists are not aware of the real reasons when choosing a particular tourism offer and that they make deci-sions subconsciously. The socio-psychological theory is opposed to psychoana-lytical theory. It denotes that social variables represent the basic determinants of tourist behaviour when choosing a particular service. The theory of personality traits assumes that specific characteristics characterise tourists. Based on this fact, it is necessary to determine the links between personality characteristics and the behaviour of tourists when choosing a particular tourism offer. Simulations predicting the reactions of target tourists are a prerequisite for pro-active management in the final stages of developing a new specialised tourism product, but also for modifications in the stage of maturity and declining demand for the same. This indicates the exceptional importance of marketing in developing specialised tourism products.

1.5. Specialised Tourism Products and Selective Forms of Tourism

Specialised tourism products are a prerequisite for the development of selective forms of tourism (Jafari & Xiao, 2021). Selective forms of tourism significantly contribute to a tourist destination's differentiation and global visibility (Cooper, 2021). As a result, developing specialised tourism products is imperative for the competitiveness and growth of the tourism economy (Buhalis & Sinarta, 2019).

Developing a selective form of tourism at the level of a tourism destination begins with developing a specialised tourism product. Only prominent tourism destinations have a sufficient budget to launch systematic projects for developing selective forms of tourism. In most tourism destinations, developing some selective forms of tourism offer begins with entrepreneurial initiatives for developing individual specialised tourism products. Due to the possibility of creating a complex selective form of tourism offer, it is advisable to think about each new specialised tourism product in the broader context already in the development phase. Specifically, to think about possible future modifications of the specialised tourism product, which would further adapt some of its variants to narrower segments of tourists. Such a focus on developing a new specialised tourism product implies the consideration of various modifications and completely new specialised tourism products that organise a specific selective form of tourism offer at the level of one destination. The organisation of a selective form of tourist offer at the level of one destination implies the expansion of the assortment of specialised tourism products in the depth of a certain category of offer. This contributes to strengthening the image of the integrated destination offer with the characteristics of a selective form of tourism offer to which specialised tourism products belong.

For example, one can take an island tourism destination that, without selective forms of tourism offered, is at a competitive disadvantage compared to destinations on the coast. Higher transfer costs to the island, more expensive utilities and other services will result in higher accommodation and food prices compared to destinations on the coast. Furthermore, destinations on the island are also more accessible, so many tourists will not even consider accommodation on the island. However, developing a selective form of tourism offer in an island destination can significantly influence the final choice of where members of a particular tourism segment will stay. The tourism segment interested in diving tourism will opt for a destination where the diving centre offers a wider range of diving tours. Island destinations are often geographically more favourable for diving tourism because many attractive diving sites are located in the immediate vicinity. Getting to the same localities from diving centres on land is more complicated and expensive, which has repercussions on the prices of diving trips. A diving centre located in an island destination should strive to expand its offer range, thereby contributing to developing a selective form of tourism offer – diving tourism. In addition to guided diving trips at sites with different contents and depths, the island diving centre should also develop other forms of diving tourism. Namely, one can offer excursions for free-breathers, diving tours intended for lovers of underwater photography, diving tours where indigenous species of aquatic flora and fauna are present, scuba diving courses, sport spearfishing courses and more. By neglecting the depth of the diving tourism offer, the island destination will not adequately use the lever to strengthen its identity based on the geographical advantages of the location or its image based on diving tourism (Armenski et al., 2012; Dwyer et al., 2004; Hosany et al., 2007).

Today, tourists follow the internet and are affirmative towards original new tourism products, especially in the quality of renowned receptive countries. But the dilemma is always present to what extent is it possible to predict the buying reactions of tourists towards new specialised tourism products? The depth of the assortment within a certain category of selective form of tourism is the assumption that the potential guest will more easily decide to stay in that particular destination. In this sense, the continuity of the development of selective forms of tourism and specialised tourism products is an important prerequisite for maintaining the destination's competitiveness and the national tourism offer (Jafari & Xiao, 2021; Nunkoo et al., 2019).

Chapter 2

Development Process of a Specialised Tourism Product

The formal process of its development begins with the idea of a potential new specialised tourism product. New ideas result from changes in tourist trends, interests, wishes and expectations of tourists. By thinking about these changes, new market opportunities are realised. This implies the materialisation of ideas of what could be offered loyal tourist to a destination and what could attract new tourism segments. Conceptualising an idea and developing a new specialised tourism product requires a systematic approach – monitoring and researching the tourism market, as well as clarifying dilemmas and doubts using marketing analysis. Although tourists loyal to a destination will mostly have an affirmative attitude towards the new offer, this is not a guarantee of long-term and sustainable commercialisation. New specialised tourism products are being developed not only to strengthen the attractiveness of the integrated destination product but also to attract new segments of tourists.

The future management activities of the specialised tourism product should not be neglected either. That is a continuous reminder of the specific offer. Given that a specialised tourism product's development and management activities imply financial investments, it needs to be carefully planned and monitored. Global tourism trends are changing with lifestyle, taste and technological environment changes. The life cycles of tourism products are shorter nowadays than they were 40 or more years ago (Jafari & Xiao, 2021). The growth of competition among receptive destinations is evident. You can compete with content, accommodation, service performance and other ways. In conditions of growth and strengthening of competition in tourism, expanding the range of offers is imperative to protect market share. Analyses and marketing tools used in developing and managing specialised tourism products are also practical for solving everyday dilemmas in the tourism business.

In developing and managing a specialised tourism product, possible useful modifications of the content of the offer are achieved by constantly monitoring tourists' reactions. The initial idea of a new specialised tourism product should be constantly evaluated and compared with similar offers from competitors. The

Specialised Tourism Products, 25–46
Copyright © 2024 Neven Šerić, Ivana Kursan Milaković and Ivan Peronja
Published under exclusive licence by Emerald Publishing Limited
doi:10.1108/978-1-83549-408-020241002

growing fragmentation of the global tourism market and the continuous expansion of the offer of specialised tourism products can act as a disincentive. Still, it should be used as an incentive to develop new ideas. The development of the idea of a potential new specialised tourism product also implies consideration of financial profitability (Meler, 2010). Each new specialised tourism product represents a contribution to the national tourist offer, especially to the exact destination offer. Regardless, a quick return on investment should be ensured according to the standards practised in the tourism business (Baker & Riley, 1994; Prideaux, 2009). The specialised tourism product should ultimately be adapted to legal, social and other norms and standards. The level of compliance contributes to its faster acceptance, whereas the practice has proven that it is also a guarantee of its long-term sustainability (Swarbrooke & Horner, 2007). From a social aspect, a specialised tourism product should be in line with the ethical standards of the target tourism and the local population of the receptive destination within which it is offered and sold (Tsung Hung, 2013; Vargas-Sanchez et al., 2011). With the development of the idea, it is necessary to simultaneously develop the marketing mix of the new specialised tourism product. The marketing mix should be based on specific tourists' needs. Any discrepancy between the new tourism product and the tourists' needs for which it is intended will have negative repercussions on the dynamics of its adoption and realised sales.

2.1. Stages of Development of a Specialised Tourism Product

Modifications of the initial idea characterise the process of developing a specialised tourism product until its final transformation into a concrete offer (Lehman & Winner, 2005). Acknowledging that tourism is a specific social phenomenon (Baggio, 2020), certain activities are different than the implementation of the process of developing tangible products. The process always starts with proposing one or more ideas for new offer. This is followed by a phase in which the ideas are analysed and some of them are decided upon. Then, a more concrete conception of potential new tourism products is defined for the selected ones. Each idea is viewed in the context of a specific marketing strategy. Now, it is possible to simulate different scenarios of commercialisation of sustainable ideas. This is how the creation of simulations of the possible sale of potential new tourism products is approached. The idea, whose viability is confirmed by the analyses, is more concretely shaped into a future specialised tourism product with all the most essential features in the next phase. This is followed by market testing, which is often carried out on one or more small groups of tourists who belong to the target segment for which the new specialised product is designed. Satisfactory market test results are a prerequisite for final commercialising of the new offer for the wider tourist population.

The idea of a potential new specialised tourism product often results from information about changes in global trends. Changes in tourists' behaviour indicate new wishes and expectations (Buhalis et al., 2019). Ideas for new specialised tourism products are also learned by analysing the existing range of destination offers. The development of a new specialised tourism product is a complex process. The initial idea should be based on relevant information about existing and potential visitors to the destination where the same is planned to be offered. Choosing and selecting ideas and developing them will ultimately affect earnings (Lehman & Winner, 2005). A similar specialised tourism product from different segments of tourists will not be accepted in the same way (Prorok et al., 2019). New specialised tourism products based on autochthonous customs and local gastronomy, which also involve the active participation of tourists, are accepted more quickly in the most economically developed emission tourism markets. In post-transition emotive tourism markets, specialised tourism products linked to global celebrities are accepted more quickly (Jafari & Xiao, 2021).

The life span of many tourism products is being shortened (WTTC, 2020). For this reason, it is recommended that the concept of developing and managing a specialised tourism product allows for the necessary modifications that implement additional features when deemed necessary. Regarding the growth of competition and the risks of copying the same ideas, it is required to speed up activities in the development process. However, the importance of each phase should not be ignored. Any idea about a potential new specialised tourism product should be gradually implemented through all eight development stages. The process proceeds according to the sequence shown in Fig. 1.

Following Kotler et al. (2010) and tourism, we can discuss two possibilities. The first is the acquisition of a new specialised tourism product. In tourism practice, this is carried out by taking over a business entity that has adequate resources (concession) or already offers specific new specialised tourism content. By taking over a business entity, the right to use the concession and all other rights is acquired. Already defined and commercialised new tourism products have a defined profit margin. Perspectives of content modification (to attract the

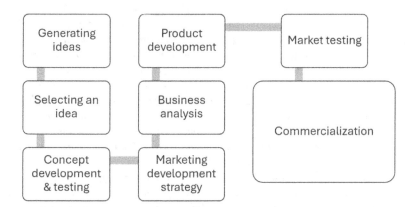

Fig. 1.   Sequence of Stages in the Development Process of a New Specialised Tourism Product. *Source:* Adapted from: Šerić (2016).

attention of additional tourist segments) are also limited (Wang, 2008). If the specialised tourism product acquired in this way is original, it should be legally protected at least at the level of the receptive tourism country. In the case of event tourism products, it is a common practice to protect them legally. These specialised tourism products are usually acquired by purchasing a license. License rights regulate the rights and obligations of the buyer/acquirer.

Another possibility of expanding the offer with new specialised tourism content is the development from idea to commercialisation. Access is implemented in tourist practice in two ways. The first way is the development of an idea by one's employees (case study 1). According to the accepted idea, it is developed within the business entity until the final offer and its commercialisation.

Case Study 1: Company X, Split, Croatia – *Split Walking Tour*

Company X was founded in 2012 in Split, Republic of Croatia, and specialised in tourism and hospitality services, especially travel agency services. To date, the company has developed several recognisable tourist brands. Its offer strives to implement innovations thanks to good differentiation and competitiveness of specialised tourism products. The company's headquarters is the Diocletian Palace Experience hospitality and business facility within the 1,700-year-old Roman Diocletian's Palace in Split. Diocletian's Wine House has a superb gastro and eno offer of more than 100 top Croatian wines. The combined modern and traditional Mediterranean cuisine attracts different tourist segments. In the gastronomic offer, in addition to entirely new and original dishes, they promote some old, already forgotten local dishes. There are nine luxuriously furnished double rooms within the building. The location was chosen because there was one of the first inns in old Split hundreds of years ago. In the fourth century AD, the stables of the Roman imperial army were located in the same area.

In order to mark the opening of a new restaurant in a specific way, the founder and owner Josip Sedlar developed and commercialised the Split walking tour project in 2007 with his colleagues. This specialised tourism product is still a recognisable tourism brand of Split on Trip Advisor. Relying on selected professional and experienced tourist guides, they have developed a wide range of specialised guided tourist walking tours. Accompanied programmes are offered in several foreign languages. Thematic tours are based on many local stories and legends of the famous 1,700-year-old history of the city of Split. The cultural–historical heritage of the town is additional content incorporated into specific stories and legends. During this specialised tourism product's development, many tourists who wander and see the city without a concrete plan were recognised. Specialised walking tours in a unique market niche offer very different thematic contents from legends and historical events, shaped into dark, sports, alternative health and other specialised tourism products. The programmes are presented in detail in illustrated brochures distributed at the reception desks of hotels and other accommodation facilities in Split and tourism spots in its surroundings. Pre-booked guests are met by qualified guides who accompany them on all walking tours at the indicated time and easily accessible locations in the city. When this specialised tourism product was commercialised, it was not clearly regulated by law, so patience was needed until the competent municipal services recognised it. Company X did not opt for legal protection of the product, considering that the competitiveness was based on the quality of the accompanying staff and the continuous addition of stories and legends of each walking tour. Over time, other travel agencies began to offer it as well. Thus, in Split today, many walking tours are provided for different tourist segments. The variety of content, duration and quality of accompanying staff covers very different needs of tourists, which ultimately contributes significantly to the promotion of the tourist destination. This is an example of the development of a specialised tourism product that greatly influenced the education of visitors to the city of Split and the strengthening of the global recognition of the destination through social networks where visitors often share experiences and many details that fascinate them during walking tours. The tourist entity has recently expanded its offer to include other guided tours. Today, Company X offers Split kayaking tours, Split snorkelling tours, Split marathon tours and other programmes. New proposals are evaluated through focus groups of connoisseurs, workshops with tourist guides and consultations with external experts in archaeology, history, marketing and tourism. Particularly desirable characteristics of walking tours for different tourist segments are selected. In creative discussions, all submitted proposals are analysed, and a team is determined to carry out the final stages of developing the new walking tour and introducing it to the market.

Another less common way to develop a new specialised tourism product under one's direction is to delegate the new idea to an outsourcing marketing agency. The agency independently carries out the development process. It delivers a study to the client within the agreed time frame for introducing and positioning the new tourism product on the market. This approach is recommended in a situation where it is a specific resource and a potential new specialised tourism product intended for a narrower segment of users. Considering the relevant capacities and accompanying resources for tourism accommodation in monasteries, this approach would be recommended for this form of religious tourism (Case study 2).

Case Study 2: The Development Potential of Monastery Tourism

The Republic of Croatia is extremely rich in monastic heritage (Šerić & Talijančić, 2011). Considering that these are valuable cultural and historical buildings requiring significant maintenance investments, they began to think about the tourism valorisation of vacant housing capacities. Previous attempts resulted from the initiatives of managers of individual monasteries (http://www.samostan-zaostrog.com/?t=G0&pg=3; https://gostinjacbsm.com/guest-houses-zadar/). Modest tourism experiences and lack of familiarity with tourism

(Continued)

(Continued)

trends generally result in a fair number of overnight stays. Considering that the offer is categorised as part of religious tourism, it tries to connect with different sacred events in the destinations or near those where these monasteries are located. This specialised tourism offer in the Republic of Croatia has only been used modestly, more symbolically. The potential is not only in providing the necessary funds for the ongoing financial maintenance of valuable cultural and historical heritage but also in the possibility of spreading Christianity and Christian culture to the broader tourist population. In the context of such goals, it is necessary to adapt the existing offer to current tourist trends regarding accommodation, food and accompanying facilities. In addition, the enthusiasm of rare individuals from church circles should be used institutionally for all monasteries that have accessible accommodation facilities. Tourism is acceptable considering the daily activities of church dignitaries who always stay there. For the further development of such a specialised tourism offer in the Republic of Croatia, it is advisable to engage a competent marketing or tourism agency. Such an agency could significantly contribute to the global visibility of another unique form of tourism offer and adequately promote another valuable national resource of the Republic of Croatia. The development and growth of the tourism offered in monasteries would fulfil one of the strategic goals of Christian communities, the spread of Christian culture and faith.

A combined approach is helpful to achieving the long-term sustainability of a specialised tourism product in developing new ideas. The combined approach implies a marketing story in which the specifics and different characteristics of a potential new specialised tourism offer are interwoven. A combined approach was used in the development of a specialised tourism product for the valorisation of Adriatic lighthouses (Šerić, 2004, 2008). This specialised tourism product is a typical example of a combination of the lighthouse tradition on the Adriatic, cultural and historical heritage, ecological preservation of the locality and basic activities related to navigation safety and adventure (Case study 3).

Case Study 3: Company Y – Tourist Stay at the Lighthouse

Lighthouses in the Republic of Croatia are managed by a state company, Company Y, from Split (the legal successor of the former Austro-Hungarian Office of Navigation Safety). During the 90s of the XX century, the lights in the lighthouses were automated, and remote monitoring was introduced. During the second half of the 20th century, the existing navigation safety system in the eastern Adriatic was improved by constructing many new coastal and harbour lights (Šerić, 2004). This system today consists of more than 1,200 objects of navigation safety (lighthouses, coastal and harbour lights, signal buoys and others). After the automation of the lighthouse lights, human crews were withdrawn from some of the lighthouses. Those were the lighthouses where keepers lived with their families, now left with professionals who perform the service in shifts of 15 or 30 days. A significant part of the residential space in the lighthouse buildings has commercialisation possibilities. Most of the lighthouse buildings represent protected national cultural heritage, limiting some opportunities for commercialisation, whereas the Republic of Croatia has not provided funds for construction maintenance. Company Y is obliged to take care only for technical equipment for the safety of navigation. Another legal problem of commercialisation was the unsettled documentation on the land ownership on which the lighthouses were built in the land registers.

Adriatic lighthouses were recognised as some destination icons. Historically, the tourism boards from Istria were leaders (the photograph of the rock with the lighthouses Porer and Sv. Ivan became a standard of tourism brochures that presented the Istrian peninsula even at a time when access to the lighthouses was strictly prohibited for tourists and other unauthorised persons).

Tourism valorisation of lighthouse buildings to solve the ongoing investment maintenance of these valuable buildings was imposed by itself, especially for lighthouses from which human crews were withdrawn after the automation of the lights. Thus, in 1995, the 'Pharos' project proposal was presented to the public. The project planned to transfer the lighthouse buildings to all interested legal and private entities for 99 years of the concession. The public did not support the project because it was considered a sale of national silver (Šerić, 2004). The problem of realising the project was also the status of cultural property for many lighthouse buildings. Such a status implies the execution of all building renovations under the supervision of conservation services following the original plans. This condition would turn away many potential investors due to the high costs. In search of another solution – the sustainable commercialisation of lighthouse buildings to secure funds for ongoing financial maintenance in 1997 – the Croatian government approved the use of the lighthouse for tourism purposes in Company Y. As a result, in 1999, the company administration accepted the proposal of the complex investment project 'Stone Lights' - tourism valorisation of lighthouse buildings. The project envisages the gradual renovation of the lighthouse buildings in which tourists' apartments would be arranged in a part of the free housing space. The project was financed partly by own funds and partly by loans. The project was designed and realised through all stages of development by Neven Šerić and Hrvoje Mandekić.

The idea was presented in 1999, and the other phases of developing the future specialised tourism product were carried out during the next 2 years. First tourism offer of staying in the lighthouse was launched in the global tourist market in 2001.

In the project's first phase, a dozen lighthouses were renovated, equipped and categorised for tourism purposes, mainly those with lighthouse crews.

(*Continued*)

(Continued)

In addition to lighthouse keepers' regular duties at the lighthouses where tourists visit, they are their hosts. Before the arrival of new guests, they arrange and clean the apartments, organise the shipment of bed linens and towels for washing and dispose of degradable waste (another waste is transported to the mainland). Hence, a narrow guest sub-segment wishes to stay at the lighthouse in complete isolation (without a lighthouse keeper) are acknowledged. In addition, several more lighthouse buildings without human crews were arranged for this purpose. The lighthouse keeper's work at these lighthouses is sporadically performed by caretakers who visit them. Automated lighthouses without human forces are near the settlements where the janitors live.

The connection of the brand 'Stone Lights - guardians of lanterns (lighthouses) of historical value' emphasised the marketing context of the commercialisation of lighthouse buildings. Despite the innovative concept of tourism valorisation and the new specialised tourism product, lighthouses, their heritage and tradition are still modestly used in the identity and image of the national tourism offer of the Republic of Croatia. The global promotion of lighthouses and lighthouse heritage is carried out independently by Company Y. During the last 10 years, the photo exhibition 'Croatian Lighthouses', which was placed in about a 100 cities worldwide, has been particularly notable.

The 'Stone Lights' brand has positioned itself on the global tourism market as an association of specific specialised tourism offers for staying at the lighthouse. Travel agencies and sales partners used the brand as original content to differentiate their offers. This can be seen in photos with lighthouse on the covers of many tourism brochures. A tourism stay at Adriatic lighthouses is recognised as a unique and exclusive experience, whereas lighthouses have become a recognisable national feature of the Republic of Croatia. Many reports were published about the project and the lighthouses in the foreign press, while several documentaries were filmed and broadcast on national television.

Case study 3 argues the importance of fully implementing the development of a potential new specialised tourism project, primarily when based on different categories of resources (cultural, historical, natural, strategic – national navigation safety, etc.).

The first phase, generating ideas about a potential new specialised tourism product, is based on the ideas and suggestions of own employees, business partners and tourists loyal to a tourism area or destination. Ideas are then analysed in focus groups. In similar offer categories, experiences of existing good tourism practices are compared. The acceptance of the same in the global tourism market is analysed. This way, potential emission tourism markets, whose clientele could be attracted by a new specialised offer, are recognised. According to the standards of the target markets, the basic characteristics of a potential new specialised tourism product are adjusted. In the second phase, elaboration and selection of ideas, experts are consulted for specific categories of special forms of tourism. Existing ideas are supplemented with content and evaluated for marketing purposes. After that, some ideas are rejected, and ideas assessed as viable are referred to the further procedure. When evaluating the ideas of a new specialised tourism product, they are categorised as uncorrectable (drop error) and correctable (go error). This is how they are classified during the following stages of development. An irreparable mistake is made when assumed that a potential new specialised tourism product will not, despite everything, attract the special attention of tourists. This questions profitability and economic justification. For example, this is a challenge due to the high costs of realising and providing a specialised tourism service, insufficiently attractive features of such an offer, the small number of tourists who could express interest in the same and the like. An example of a potential new specialised tourism product from the authors' practice is presented in Case study 4.

Case Study 4: *Extreme Adriatic Warrior* – **Extreme Team Building**

In 2002, the first author of this book was engaged in analysing and evaluating the profitability of a proposal to commercialise a new specialised tourism product – 'Extreme Adriatic Warrior'. Two international military instructors developed the concept of specific team-building content as an entrepreneurial idea in Croatia. Based on many years of military experience, they designed a programme that would offer experiences of actual military operations without using real arms. The contents and attractive locations where the programme would take place differentiated it from the current offers of war games based on paintball and airsoft. Content and intensity of efforts for participants of different programme versions lasting from 7 to 21 days were analysed. The programme included several specialist instructors (diving, climbing and survival in nature) and other support staff (nurses/paramedics) and technical means (helicopter, self-propelled combat vehicle, motorised flying kites, pneumatic boat, etc.). In addition to these costs, the financial calculation also included insurance policies for participating tourists to protect against possible financial lawsuits for damages due to accidents and incidents. The programme could be acceptable to a more affluent tourist clientele regarding the estimated costs. After covering the anticipated costs, the profit margin was assessed as satisfactory. Concept testing of this offer was carried out with a multimedia animated presentation on a small sample of potential tourists.

It was determined that tourists for this offer should be in good physical condition due to the programme implementation's expected dynamics to carry out all the planned activities. A high risk for some participants dropping out during the programme was assessed. The same was approached as a risk of negative publicity, reducing the number of new interested tourists. Alternatively, simplifying the programme's content would reduce the offer's differentiation

(Continued)

(Continued)

compared to the usual paintball and airsoft activities. The reach of specific locations that contributed to the attractiveness of the potential offer would also be limited. It was concluded that to participate in this type of tourism arrangement successfully, the participating tourists should spend several days in a preparatory camp. However, the concept of a boot camp (with a programme of exercises practised in American military camps based on the use of one's weight and body resistance) was still unknown in Europe at that time. In addition, such preparation of the tourism programme participants would extend the overall arrangement duration. As a result of all these findings, the 'Extreme Adriatic Warrior' programme was rated as a drop error, so further development was abandoned.

From today's perspective, it can be concluded that the creators of the idea of this specialised tourism product were ahead of their time. Boot camp appeared as a specific tourism offer in Europe only in 2005. The concept of 'Extreme Adriatic Warrior' was more complex and advanced. If the creators had based the idea of a new specialised tourism product on the content of the boot camp, they might have been recorded as the first to offer such thing in Europe. Regardless of the 'Extreme Adriatic Warrior programme' commercialisation abandonment due to its complexity and completeness, it is still studied in the marketing courses of the graduate study of tourism at the University of Split.

Case study 4 argues that the determination of a drop error (uncorrectable error) should be understood as a sign to give up on the idea. But the case study also points to the possibility that within the idea of a complex, specialised tourism product, there is also a simpler version that is perhaps more rational for commercialisation (boot camp).

The third stage of developing a new specialised tourism product continues if it is concluded that the idea has a market perspective despite certain weaknesses. In this phase, the development and testing of the concept of a new specialised tourism product, the features and content are elaborated in more detail. Based on the detailed elaboration of the idea, several different conceptions of the potential new product are defined. They are ranked according to the criterion of attractiveness for specific tourist segments. Different matrices are used for this purpose, which will be discussed in more detail later. Multivariate analysis or some other method should be used to evaluate several characteristics. A simpler tool for evaluating two fundamental features of different concepts of a new specialised tourism product is the perception map presented in Fig. 2. Based on the mutual comparison, the two best-rated concepts are selected for further development (in the map, they tend to the upper right corner of the upper right quadrant of the perception map, i.e. concepts marked with six-pointed stars).

Fig. 2 shows the working perception map used in ranking eight conceptions of the idea of a potential new specialised tourism product in one of the author's

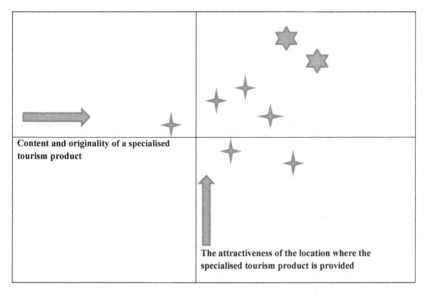

Fig. 2.   Perceptual Map in the Third Stage of the Development
Process of a New Specialised Tourism Product. *Source:* Authors' research
(2019).

researches. The basic characteristics according to which the concepts were evaluated in this research were as follows:

- The attractiveness of the location where the specialised tourism product would
  be offered (e.g. right next to the sea, located on the lower side of the road by the
  sea, located on the upper side of the road, on the slopes of a nearby hill, at a
  viewpoint).
- Originality and attractiveness of the characteristics of different conceptions of a
  potential new specialised tourism product.

Based on these characteristics, the table ranks eight concepts of a new specialised tourism product, six four-pointed stars and two six-pointed options that
will continue to develop.

In the fourth stage of the new product development process, the design of the
marketing strategy and the development of proposed tactics to implement it
begin. By this stage, potential tourist segments that could be interested and
attracted by a new specialised tourism product have already been identified. Based
on these findings, a promotional mix is developing. The same will be used to
communicate the new specialised tourism product. In this phase, the existing
specialised tourism products that represent competition to the new tourism offer
should be evaluated. A price strategy is planned based on these findings. The
established marketing strategy is modified and adapted in the following stages of

developing a new specialised tourism product following new market knowledge. Attention should be paid to how the target tourist clientele reacts to the content of the specialised tourism offer, whether the price is acceptable to them, how they perceive the staff serving them, etc. The marketing strategy of the specialised tourism product should be aligned with the set mission and vision. The effectiveness of the marketing strategy of a new specialised tourism product depends on the adaptation to the market and ethical standards in the target emission markets. The fifth stage of developing a new specialised tourism product involves business analysis simulations. Based on these analyses, quantitative estimates of possible sales are made. The total costs of the new specialised tourism product are estimated. The potential earnings and dynamics of return on investment in developing and commercialising a new specialised tourism product are determined.

Product development's sixth phase implies the final design of a new specialised tourism product. At this stage, the new offer includes all the characteristics and logistics of the provision. All decisions are discussed with partners and stakeholders involved in promoting, selling and providing a new specialised tourism service. The new specialised tourism offer is presented to stakeholders and partners but not yet to tourists. Based on stakeholders' impressions in this testing, individual features are modified, and the optimal duration of a new tourism service provision is estimated (duration of excursions, events, etc.). The phase is also concluded with the decision to introduce and position the new specialised tourism product on the market. With the findings of the sixth phase, the prerequisites for testing a new specialised tourism product on a smaller sample of tourists have been achieved. Existing tourist clientele loyal to the destination or a hotel complex is usually selected. Tourists selected for the test sample are also presented as a kind of reward for loyalty. It is important to carry out the testing so that the new offer is not overexposed to the competition. Based on the impressions and comments of tourists on whom the new product was tested, the final modifications of individual features are made. The dynamics of introducing a new offer to the market are also determined, and sales policies are decided upon. Sales agents and promoters were also selected. The promotion plan (set in the previous phase as part of the marketing strategy) is concluded.

The final stage of the process of developing a new specialised tourism product is commercialisation, i.e. introduction to the market. It decides where the same will be offered, in what terms and periods the staff is selected and more. Based on the marketing mix, future management activities of the new specialised tourism product are being elaborated. Attitudes and reactions of tourists to the new specialised tourism offer indicate whether the process of development so far has been carried out under marketing standards. Quick acceptance and loyalty to a new specialised tourism product is a confirmation of a job well done, that is, the recognition and attractiveness of the offer.

2.2. Practice of Tourism Destinations

Mediterranean countries did not plan or systematically develop specialised tourism products. Tourism development in the Mediterranean coastal countries took place according to inertia, stimulated by the growth of tourist visits. Motivated by profit goals, local tourism stakeholders offered new content by commercialising available resources. Without respecting the standards of responsible and sustainable tourism, such practice of tourism development resulted in the uncontrolled consumption of many non-renewable natural resources (Šerić, Peronja, et al., 2020). The mentioned authors question how much this has contributed to lowering the competitiveness of coastal tourism destinations in the Eastern Adriatic. In addition, the authors determined the importance and contribution of specialised tourism content to the competitiveness of the integrated offer of the tourism destination (Šerić, 2019b; Šerić & Batalić, 2018; Šerić & Marušić, 2019; Šerić & Meža, 2014). The management of the integrated destination product (the entire tourism offer of the destination) can be effectively implemented with different policies for the sale of specialised tourism products. Such an approach can influence content's higher or lower attractiveness, primarily depending on the price of the offers. Originality and the intensity of its promotion contribute to the attractiveness of a specialised tourism product. Today, tourism stakeholders are aware of the contribution of specialised tourism products to the destination's competitiveness, so they encourage their development. Just as all activities of managing the tourism development of a destination need to be planned, the same standards should be applied in developing new specialised tourism products.

Regarding the tourism practice of most Mediterranean destinations, there was an unsystematic valorisation of many valuable resources to commercialise mostly straightforward specific tourism content. Rampant commercialisation, especially of landscape resources, endangers them and rapidly diminishes their value. In such situations, it is advisable to introduce special regulations that would suspend the commercialisation of particularly endangered resources in specific periods and thus enable their renewal. Another justification for such consideration is that many specialised tourism products are market obsolete, and modifications and improvements are necessary. Maintaining the existing state of offers of specialised tourism products often means offering them at low penetration prices. Despite such a pricing strategy, tourists' interest in them is declining. Such specialised tourism products are in the graveyard zone (Šerić, Jakšić Stojanović, et al., 2023), while maintaining demand for them implies a low price. Such a practice in tourism entrepreneurship is often accompanied by tax evasion to obtain some profit. That is why it is not in the interest of local self-government units to maintain such tourist facilities. The same can be practically regulated by introducing restrictions/higher concession prices for the use of significantly burdened resources (Šerić & Luković, 2013).

In modern marketing practice, one of the solutions is the *rejuvenation* of a specialised tourism product. Rejuvenation implies changes in the features of the specialised tourism offer and expansion of its content. Rejuvenation of a specialised tourism product has been successfully implemented when a new life cycle of a modified tourist offer is launched. Regardless, it is important to monitor the state of the resources on which the specialised tourism product is based, accounting for a responsible and sustainable valorisation (Šerić, Pavlinović, et al., 2011). Monitoring the state of resources implies a multidisciplinary approach and respect for the views of experts from different fields (biology, geography, oceanography, urbanism and spatial planning, etc.). Rejuvenation of existing and development of new specialised tourism products are prerequisites for the sustainable development of the tourism destinations' economy. These activities also affect the structure of the tourism destination's visitors. Namely, clientele with higher out-of-board spending prefers original tourism facilities, high ecological standards and sustainable management of destination resources. The management of developing the destination's specialised tourism products should also be coordinated with the set goals of tourism development. Such synergy aligns the consumption of precious destination resources with the vision of the tourism future.

In the ranking and selection of proposals for the improvement of existing and development of new specialised tourism products, knowledge about the experiences of others based on scouting and benchmarking research can be used (Šerić & Jurišić, 2014). It is practical to analyse selected specialised tourism products using the BCG matrix. Such categorisation also provides additional insights into the long-term sustainability of specialised tourism content. Content that needs to be further modified (cash cows and stars), content that should perhaps (question marks) or definitely (dogs) should be abandoned primarily because of their negative repercussions on the destination's non-renewable resources, is noticed on time. Fig. 3 shows the BCG matrix from the author's research.

STARS	QUESTION MARKS
Gastronomic musical evenings; Guided diving visits to underwater sites with indigenous flora and fauna; Paddleboarding - routes under the cliffs near the destination	Gastronomic workshops *from field to table*; Schools of autonomous diving; Rides in a mini-submarine with a glass bottom; Classical music evenings
CASH COWS	DOGS
Photo safari at viewpoints; Simple recreational sports facilities; Bicycle rental on organised bicycle paths; Rental of motor and rubber boats	Offer intended for sailors on a transit connection; Hiking and hiking trails

Fig. 3.   Presentation of the BCG Matrix of Specialised Tourism Products of *Destination X. Source:* Authors (2018).

Comment on the Distribution of Tourism Products in the BCG Matrix of Destination X

The income from sailors staying at the transit connection to the destination is negligible. Boaters decide to spend the night there because there are no coves in the area where they could anchor safely during the night. Records show that they only stay one night in transit and rarely go out in the evening. Since the price of the transit connection is low, this income is negligible. In addition, the possibility of discharging sanitary wastewater from the vessel's tanks should not be ignored. By ending the possibility of boaters staying overnight at the transit link in the destination, given the relief of the surrounding coast and the absence of nautical ports, the number of boaters in the surrounding waters would be significantly reduced, which would have positive effects on sea pollution due to the discharge of waste hygienic water from ships.

Free movement along the hiking and hiking trails on the nearby mountain results in extraordinary costs due to the search for tourists who go for a walk on the mountain alone, unprepared and without experience. The introduction of guided walking and climbing tours that connect attractive localities on the mountain would increase the tourism income of the destination, encourage new employment and self-employment and reduce the costs of searching for missing and lost tourists. The specialised destination's tourism products, categorised as stars and cash cows, indicate an essential thing. They point out why some aspects should be expanded with additional content, e.g. autonomous diving schools, gastronomic workshops based on harvesting and preparation of indigenous foods, glass-bottomed mini-submarine rides without concrete contents for sightseeing and classical music evenings in this destination. For instance, this can be done by connecting sporadic evenings of classical music into a festival event through which the works of different composers originating from strategic tourism countries would be presented every summer. The autonomous diving school could be relocated from the city beach due to the sandy and unattractive underwater to a location with a more attractive underwater relief. Gastronomic workshops could be tied thematically with the target tourist population, e.g. vegans, vegetarians, Mediterranean spices lovers, etc. One could organise rides in a mini submarine with a glass bottom at a specific location with concrete content in the sea or even sink some dilapidated indigenous wooden ship.

Tourism facilities are generally classified as dogs since there is an evident endangerment and consumption of a destination resource. In the sequence, they generate a modest or no income. Often, such tourism facilities in destinations result from former trends and habits of tourists who stayed in the destination in previous decades. In the survey of attitudes, tourists pointed out that the offer of gastronomic workshops from field to table should be adapted to different dietary concepts (e.g. traditional Mediterranean diet, vegan diet, raw food offer, etc.). Tourists who stay at the destination do not favour the diving school held on the main beach in the place and think that this activity should be relocated. Because

(Continued)

(Continued)

of this attitude, some tourists who would have enrolled in a diving school in another location give up on this idea. Guided diving tours also attract recreational divers because they feel safe, and the specifics of individual diving locations generate the impression of the more added value of the offer. Connecting local gastronomy with autochthonous music contributes to the overall experience of such tourism facilities. The promotion of recreational paddle boarding along the route under the nearby cliffs further adds to the appeal of today's standard offer. Among cash cows, one should recognise those whose life cycle is potentially coming to an end, so they should be enriched with additional content.

Controlled consumption of available non-renewable resources imposes the need to design additional substantive features that would strengthen the appeal of a specialised tourism product. In the research carried out by the authors, most of the existing specialised tourism products in destination X were qualified by respondents as insufficiently attractive for repeated purchases during their stay in the destination. The surveyed tourists who recognised the first experience as something new after what they had experienced did not remember anything that would encourage them to buy that tourist service again during the following days of their stay in the same destination. Good global practice suggests using different replicas (archaeological, etc.) to enhance the experience of diving tours, walking and cycling routes. Connecting specific locations with the stories and legends can also stimulate additional ideas that would contribute to the authenticity of the site where the specialised tourism product is offered. For instance, artificial human skeletons placed on the bottom of the sea, feeders for wild animals and underwater fauna for photo safaris, etc.

Music events are a real tourist attraction if speaking of the global stars. The engagement of artists in this category generates high costs, so it is not an economically rational solution for many smaller tourism destinations. Based on autochthonous music performed by local musicians, musical events can attract a wider tourist population only if other autochthonous contents, such as gastronomic, recreational or other, are connected with it. The findings of the author's research indicate that tourists rate gastronomic musical evenings as an original event, considering the thematic connection of the musical content with the gastronomic offer. In addition, guided diving visits to the remains of a shipwreck and the guided dive into an underwater cave were also considered attractive by the surveyed tourists. Diving tours around the underwater wreck can be organised with different content variants. Moreover, each of them could imply a different perspective and tour of the underwater site. Furthermore, various sunken reliefs, such as characteristic aquatic flora and fauna specimens, will contribute to different impressions. In addition, it will encourage new dives in the same location. For instance, at an underwater location on the island of Vis in Croatia, the concessionaire connects the story with the identical approach and perspective of the shipwreck with the surprise feeding of a large eel that lives in the immediate vicinity. Every dive is similar. In tourist seasons with many tourists, the concessionaire will be satisfied with the total visit. But in the pre-season and post-season, the number of dives decreases because the monotony of the diving scenario rarely encourages tourists to repeat the same experience.

Tourists primarily choose paddle boarding for recreational reasons. Offering specific thematic rowing coastal routes with information about the content that can be seen and experienced contributes to the impression of the higher value of the provided specialised tourism product, which is the assumption of higher equipment rental prices. Photo safaris at viewpoints, mini golf and table tennis and rental of bicycles and motor and rubber boats have generated high tourism traffic in destination X during the primary tourism season in recent years. However, the more affluent tourism clientele does not perceive these facilities as particularly attractive despite the relatively low prices (compared to the prices of the same offer in globally known summer resorts). These types of tourism offer show a growth trend, which results in lower prices, except during the primary tourist season when there are days when the demand for these contents is greater than the available capacities of the offer.

The profit margins of specialised tourism products that do not introduce content extensions have decreased in recent years. This is also a consequence of the growth of competition. Still, the tourists are always ready to pay more for a specific tourism service in which they recognise the concrete added value. The higher quality of provision provides added value to all tourism services. Still, in the case of specialised tourism products, the expanded content significantly contributes to the experience of added value. Content expansions and improvements encourage additional interest for more frequent purchases to repeat the experience. Content modifications of specialised tourism products categorised into *question marks* will determine their future. All specialised tourism products classified as dogs, if they are still not particularly attractive to tourists after modifying the content, are economically unjustified and should be eliminated from the destination's offer.

Continuity of provision should be enabled for all specialised tourism products that show *star* characteristics in the destination offer, as they significantly contribute to the tourist image. A *star* product/service is characterised by the possibility of increasing the profit margin and growth in demand. Maintaining the expressed high interest of tourists presupposes improvement and expansion of content for this category as well – destinations with a preserved landscape prospect of expanding the offer of *stars* in sports and recreational activities. By increasing the content of such offers and connecting them with gastronomy and local customs, the perspective of competitiveness of such offers and the destination as a whole grows significantly. Specialised tourism products categorised as *cash cows* are often components of the traditional offer with attractive prices. This segment of the destination offer also represents the predominant share, but the sales growth rates of *cash cows* are low. They can be stimulated either by price reductions (profit margins) or significant content modifications. Modifications of the *cash cow* content of specialised tourism products should be based exclusively on global tourism trends (Šerić & Jurišić, 2015). Modifications to the content of *cash cows* can be successfully carried out by changing the place, method and personnel who provide them. Accompanying facilities for *cash cows* in tourism can also provide new youth.

The *question marks* in the destination offer include specialised tourism products that tourists choose sporadically. It is possible that the demand for the same offers is growing in the global tourism market, but it needs to be determined in which emission markets. It is often not a general trend, but the growth of interest is expressed in emerging markets whose tourists have recognised such offers as some specific links with their culture and national value standards. In such emission markets, *question marks* can be transformed into *stars*. It is possible to speed up the transformation if the specialised tourism offer is adapted to the preferences of tourists from these emission markets with additional features (new trends for specific services and overall content).

Specialised tourism products that show the characteristics of a *dog* at the destination level are often the result of economically unjustified local institutional support for individual entrepreneurs. Economically, they do not justify maintenance in the destination offer. In some destinations, such specialised tourism products result from tradition, but without local support and co-financing, they would not be maintained. The maintenance of such contents in the destination offer is justified only if they are based on the destination's identity. Then they can be used for repositioning and rebranding the destination to strengthen global visibility. If they do not have links with the identity and icons of the destination, the only rational solution for maintaining such content is modification and harmonisation with current tourism trends.

The analysis of the structure of the destination's integrated tourism offer provides insight into the substantive participation of various categories of specialised tourism products. Tourism practice shows that the growth of annual visits and the extension of the tourism season depends on the share of such content (Barros & Alves, 2004; Bi et al., 2011; Botti et al., 2009; Hadad et al., 2012; Tomic & Marcikic Horvat, 2016; Šerić, 2012b; Šerić, Jakšić Stojanović, et al., 2023).

The existing tourism infrastructure and destination logistic support are important for developing new and managing existing specialised tourism products (approvals and regulations related to using specific resources – concessions). One-dimensional conclusions based on an insight into the BCG matrix are not recommended, especially if specialised tourism products are in different phases of the life cycle (the stage they are currently in can have a significant impact on their current position in the BCG matrix) (Šerić, 2016).

When analysing specialised tourism offer as a whole, each content should be evaluated by its share at the level of the destinations, considering the totality of all tourism content. Competitiveness can be measured by the breadth and quality of the content and the level of the possible premium addition to the price. In the context of the integrated destination product, the concrete contribution of the specialised tourism offer to the attractiveness of the destination and year-round tourist visits is analysed. Specialised tourism products that do not make a significant contribution according to the BCG matrix need to be categorised as *dogs*, which is another argument against their further maintenance in the destination offer, especially if they are subsidised by local authority.

Based on the analysis of the assortment of the destination's specialised tourism offers, it is possible to make economically justified decisions on support for priority contents, which are often catalysts for tourism growth. With such contents, it is justified to strengthen the logistic support as this will affect the sales volume. The exact contents are a valuable starting point for developing new specialised tourism products. It is useful to compare the findings of analyses carried out at the destination level with the experiences of other destinations in the area. Relevant insights into one's competitiveness are gained and are helpful when making strategic guidelines in managing tourism development.

Comparing the matrices of specialised tourism products of competing destinations, one determines who manages this offer segment more efficiently. The good practice of other destinations should be evaluated in its applicability, considering the overall potential of the necessary resources for a specialised tourism offer. When making decisions about developing new specialised tourism products of the destination, one should test ideas depending on the thoughts of tourists loyal to the destination and the local population's affirmative attitudes towards tourism. Tourists loyal to a destination are glad to comment on the ideas about new content. By surveying this segment of tourists, it is possible to find out what should be additionally adapted to the current offer. Tourists loyal to a destination will also point to those that do not meet their expectations or even damage the destination's image.

Pricing decisions are crucial in managing new specialised tourism products (Hooley et al., 2004; Šerić & Luetić, 2016). It is advisable to analyse the issue of the price of a new specialised tourism product during all phases of its development. At the same time, customised pricing policies are also being developed concerning their influence when making a purchase decision. A specialised tourism product is worth as much as the target tourist is willing to pay (Šerić, 2016). One should learn from own and others' mistakes. All available information on the receptive tourist market can be used to consider pricing strategies and policies (Doyle, 2002). The price of a new specialised tourism product should be an incentive for purchase in the phase of its introduction to the market. Different categories of specialised tourism products imply different pricing strategies. The price should match the expectations of the target tourism segment following their perception of the new specialised tourism offer. Similar to brand loyalty, tourists loyal to a destination express an emotional incentive for a trial buy of something new in the offer (Jobber, 2001; Šerić, 2016; Šerić, Vitner Marković, et al., 2017). Tourists loyal to the destination subconsciously develop frequent positive associations with the new contents of the destination (Šerić, Jakšić Stojanović, et al., 2023). When managing the price strategy and policies, one should consider not undermining the affirmative attitudes of tourists loyal to the destination. In practice, accepting a new tourism product significantly depends on assessing what is received for what is paid.

2.3. Segmentation of the Global Tourism Market

The process of market segmentation begins at the idea generation stage. One should recognise segments of tourist that could be attracted. The total tourist population interested in visiting a specific destination can be classified according their needs, desired quality standards, family income, average non-boarding consumption and other criteria. By segmenting the strategic emission markets for the destination, one obtains helpful information to understand the behaviours and reactions of different groups of tourists. Based on the knowledge gathered, a decision is made for a narrower segment to which the new specialised tourism product will be primarily adapted. In addition, the promotional package should be adapted to the same segment. This mainly refers to the selection of promotional channels for which the target segment of tourists shows a particular interest. All strategic decisions in managing a new specialised tourism product during the entire life cycle should be based on knowledge about the market behaviour of the target segment (Fleisher & Bensoussan, 2003; Kerin & Peterson, 2004).

According to the previously mentioned authors, they segment the tourist market for decision-making on developing new specialised tourism products according to the characteristics that connect the specifics of the specific offer, the reasons for choosing them and the perception of the expected quality of service and content. They suggest that researchers develop their own experimental approach according to the niche in which they aim to position a new specialised tourism product. The authors use the following approaches in the segmentation of tourists to select a strategic profile:

- By geographic regions from which the targeted tourists come, considering their active participation in the provision of a specialised tourism product.
- By psychographic characteristics (social stratum to which they belong, style and way of life, personal characteristics, etc.) related to the basic content of the specialised tourism product.
- By demographic characteristics (gender, age, number of family members, education, occupation, race, ethnicity) concerning the additional content of the specialised tourism product.
- According to typical behaviours during a stay (structure of non-boarding consumption, methods of consumption, arguments on which the selection of specialised tourism products is based, loyalty to touristic brands, attitudes about specific categories of tourism products, etc.) to determine the price strategy and price policies in the sale of the specialised tourism product.

While segmenting, one should analyse the target tourism market from the perspective of business customers, meaning not only from the aspect of emitting and receptive travel agencies or tour operators, but one should also consider other business entities given the growth of interest in traditional team-building gatherings, conferences and other forms of organised demand for stays in destinations with specialised tourism facilities. Segmentation of business customers in the tourism market is often practised according to geographical (where they are registered) and substantive criteria (their interests). When making decisions about new specialised tourism facilities intended for business customers, some beneficial characteristics can be annual income, care for own employees, etc. (Fletcher, 2003). Authors use several models when segmenting the specific tourism market, such as the *classic model*, *market research model* and *combined model*. The classic model is based on the typical characteristics of the market (geographical and demographic data), after which additional necessary data are collected to adjust the final conception of the specialised tourism product. Segmentation by conducting market research implies the classification of potential buyers of new tourism content into groups of similar behaviour, structure and level of non-boarding consumption, interests, etc. The combined model implies the classification of potential buyers of a new tourism product according to one (or more) demographic and one additional characteristic. Suppose it is a more complex and expensive specialised tourism product (e.g. in health tourism). In that case, psychographic segmentation is recommended – according to the social conditions, personality and lifestyle of tourists (Šerić & Jurišić, 2014). An alternative is a behavioural segmentation, which is carried out according to the following criteria:

- Circumstances that may contribute to the demand for a particular specialised tourism product (e.g. post-pandemic times generate an increase in demand for all contents that directly contribute to immunity and health).
- Perception of the expected benefit from a specialised tourism product (in a situation of evident competitiveness of tourism destinations in the environment).
- The status of potential tourist consumers (has such a category of tourism offer already been encountered, was it preferred, can this tourist become a regular consumer, etc.).
- Frequency of purchase of a specialised tourism product and assessment of the intensity of its demand (depending on the complexity of the content, the intensity of tourist's physical and emotional efforts in obtaining, price, etc.).
- Loyalty to a touristic brand or a tourism entity that provides a specific tourism service (tourists loyal to a destination can be adamant, divided, wavering or unattached towards the provider of a new specialised tourism service).
- Motives for choosing a specialised tourism product (reasons for choosing a new specialised tourism product).
- Speed of acceptance and adoption of new specialised tourism products (impression of added value and all benefits).

During the tourist market segmentation, one should also consider the marketing strategy. The tactics used to implement the strategy refer to practical means of harmonising the features of the new specialised tourism product given the expectations and wishes of the target tourists. Certain tactics can be used to attract some currently invisible segments of tourists. In this regard, one should determine what drew their attention and affirmative reactions to the new specialised tourism offer. The implementation and adjustment of the marketing strategy in the process of segmentation of the tourist market contribute to the attractiveness of the new specialised tourism product (Šerić, 2016; Šerić & Jurišić, 2014).

Segmentation is also desirable to determine the facts contributing to tourists' loyalty to a destination. After identifying tourists loyal to a certain category of specialised tourism offer, it is possible to comprehend the causal factors contributing to this. The authors practice *mass, differentiated* or *targeted segmentation* (Šerić & Jurišić, 2014). Mass approach refers to the adaptation of the concept of a new specialised tourism product to a broader tourist population (wholly new and original tourism content that does not imply a particular psychophysical condition of the target tourist). The advantage of the approach is the possibility of faster growth in sales of specialised tourism products. Weakness is the perception of similarity of new content with some existing content. A differentiated approach implies focusing on specific characteristics of a new specialised tourism product. The primary focus is on features that significantly contribute to the differentiation of content from competitive offers with similar purposes and targeting similar tourist segments. Here, it is rational to offer two or more variations of a specialised tourism product of different characteristics, quality and content. For instance, it could be a guided diving tour, one tour visiting sunken wrecks – ambient photography, and the other visiting underwater localities with distinctive flora and fauna – macro photography. The characteristics and ways of managing each variant's marketing mix are adapted to a particular tourist segment. For example, in the specific case of tours that assume macro photography, older and more experienced divers in underwater photography are selected according to age. A differentiated approach can also be applied given the price sensitivity of individual tourist segments (the duration of the diving tour from the example). If the target tourist segments for different options are relatively homogeneous, their communication can be uniform.

The authors practice a targeted approach for specific tourism products that they assume will be accepted by only a small number of tourists (summering at the lighthouse). Tourists choose specific specialised tourism products for status (limited accommodation capacity at lighthouses) and some unique features (staying in secluded cultural and historical heritage buildings). Triggers for reservation can be subconscious (e.g. ego, challenge). A targeted segmentation tourist market approach for new specialised tourism content is a true marketing challenge offering a marketing illusion. After all, with complex specialised tourism products, the dilemma is always where the reality of the experience ends and where the illusion begins. Tourists recognise this as added value.

Chapter 3

Development of Ideas and Concepts

3.1. Origin and Development of Ideas

The process of developing a new specialised tourism product begins with the initiative of proposing ideas on innovating an existing or offering a new specialised tourism service. The idea of improving (expanding content, for example) the existing tourism offer or developing a completely new one is economically justified if adapted to some unsatisfied needs of tourists. Modifying the existing tourism offer and commercialising new specialised tourism products attracts additional attention from the tourist public and sales intermediaries. In addition, some stakeholders will recognise this as the possibility for new cooperation of mutual benefit. However, some local tourism stakeholders may perceive the commercialisation of new specialised tourism content in the destination as an attack on their offer. Innovating an existing or introducing a completely new specialised tourism service is not a guarantee of its acceptance by the target tourism clientele. Hence, it should be noted that the attractiveness of a potential new specialised tourism product will depend on its compliance with current tourism trends and the target tourist segment's perception of what is being offered.

The reasons for the continuous generation of new ideas for the improvement of the specialised tourism offer and the introduction of new contents are the following: the changes in tourism trends, the growth of competition at the level of each tourist destination and the increasing awareness of tourists about everything that is offered on the global tourism market. Modifying the existing specialised tourism offer of the destination is also justified to manage the resources used for this purpose more rationally. Expanding the content of the specialised destination offer also supports the loyalty of the existing tourism clientele. In some cases, new specialised tourism facilities aligned with responsible and sustainable tourism standards can also enable obtaining dedicated grants from European Union funds.

A new specialised tourism product is an idea of new content that could attract existing and new tourists. The economic viability of a new idea depends on its compatibility with specific tourist needs. The findings of the author's recent

Specialised Tourism Products, 47–55

Copyright © 2024 Neven Šerić, Ivana Kursan Milaković and Ivan Peronja

Published under exclusive licence by Emerald Publishing Limited

doi:10.1108/978-1-83549-408-020241003

research (on the coastal areas of the Republic of Croatia and Montenegro) indicate that the commercialisation of new specialised tourism products encourages the attention of the global tourism public and the tourism development of the destination. Financial risk always exists because new content may not attract tourists, but conservative thinking about maintaining the existing structure of the destination offer does not lead to anything better. No new content in the destination offer can only maintain guest loyalty by lowering prices. Tourists today expect constant growth in the quality and content of the destination offers. An attractive specialised tourism product results from a creative and detailed idea. The fact that, despite everything, some new specialised tourism products do not attract tourists encourages the research of such negative phenomena. What is the secret of specialised tourism products that show a trend of sales growth and the maintenance of that trend? Many authors have analysed this phenomenon (Fletcher, 2003; Grbac et al., 2008; Jakšić Stojanović & Šerić, 2018; Lockwood, 2009, etc.).

Facts from their researches indicate the need to continuously generate argumentative, potentially valuable ideas for new specialised tourism content. It is important that local government, especially local tourist offices, encourage the generation of ideas for new specialised tourism products and encourage investments in this segment of the destination tourism offer.

The existing assortment of specialised tourism products of the destination lives its life cycle, so it needs to be renewed. Ideas about new specialised tourism products are also encouraged by tourists. It is necessary to analyse their impressions and impressions during their stay at the destination. It is useful to conduct continuous surveys, especially with tourists who have affirmative attitudes towards new tourism experiences. One should analyse the idea of a new specialised tourism product in the context of the tourist segment that such content could attract. The dilemmas are always regarding the specific characteristics of new tourism content and adaptation to the target segment of tourists (Pride & Ferrell, 2000; Rocco & Hodak, 2013; Rocco & Pisnik, 2014; Šerić, 2016). The sales potential should also be evaluated when thinking about a potential new specialised tourism product. In terms of content, complex tourism products imply a more extended development period and higher costs, so market acceptance and good sales dynamics are vital. There are also dilemmas when choosing the optimal market niche. A more straightforward idea allows for more modifications during development and a more significant cost impact.

When one resolves the dilemmas about the idea of a new tourism product, it becomes clearer how to position it on the market (category of specialised tourism offer, target clientele, etc.). Good and economically viable ideas for new specialised tourism products are often the result of the interaction of stakeholders in the value chain (entrepreneurs, employees who will participate in the provision of the new service, partners in execution and sales, local tourist office as a promoter, etc.). That is why it is suitable for these stakeholders to be involved at this stage of generating ideas about a new specialised tourism product.

One can also generate ideas by analysing the existing integrated destination offer. In this way, new niches of existing tourism offers are observed. Insights into

tourists' reactions to similar categories of specialised tourism products in destinations reveal preferences for distinctive features of specific content. Benchmarking is also practical, where existing concepts of specialised tourism products
in other destinations are analysed in the context of their resources and capabil-
ities. Practical ideas will sometimes be suggested by sales agencies, tour operators
and others who are aware that introducing certain new tourism content would
strengthen the destination's competitiveness. New ideas can also be found on
social networks, especially in the comments of those who continuously stay in the
same destinations and in the discussions of tourists who exchange personal
experiences about specialised tourism products.

3.2. Evaluation and Analysis of Sustainable Ideas

Expanding the content of the destination offer is a prerequisite for maintaining
attractiveness and competitiveness. For the development and evaluation of new
ideas at the level of the tourism stakeholder to be implemented, the support of all
involved legal and natural persons is essential. Larger tourism entities (e.g. hotel
complexes) carry out this phase systematically, but employees accustomed to the
existing offer are generally not affirmative of new ideas. This results in frequent
comments, such as our guests will not be interested in it; it does not fit into our
current offer; such offer is *nothing special*, etc. Negative comments should be
excluded from the further process of evaluating ideas about a new specialised
tourism product because such comments burden the team responsible for developing a new specialised tourism offer. The risk is a fact, but expanding tourism
content is a prerequisite for maintaining the destination's attractiveness and
receptive tourism entity. Elaborating new ideas on the unfulfilled expectations of
visitors to the destination significantly reduces the risk of failure. One can further
reduce the risk of failure if the idea of a new specialised tourism product is
adapted to the needs of the target tourist segment and not to the needs of the
existing assortment of the subject's tourist offer.

Ideas are generated by a selective or non-selective approach. A selective
approach implies comparing a sample of similar specialised tourism products. The
non-selective approach has no such limitation but selects based on a sample of
very different specialised tourism products. A selective approach is recommended
given the competitiveness of the destination offer in the environment of a rich and
varied tourism offer. A non-selective approach is advised for destinations with
modest non-boarding offers and in a scenario where additional attention from the
tourist public is sought (unusual and atypical tourist content). The authors
practice a non-selective approach using generic benchmarking (Šeric, Peronja,
et al., 2020). For this purpose, *brainstorming* and *brainwriting* with local tourism
workers of various professions and specialities are practical. Suppose the same is
carried out within tourist entities. In that case, a practical solution is establishing a
particular internal forum where employees and partners (sales intermediaries)
record and comment on ideas for new specialised tourism products.

Other methods from the literature refer to *value analysis, feature analysis, Delphi method,* etc. (Lockwood, 2009; Rocco & Hodak, 2013). Considering the specifics of the post-COVID-19 era and the consequences of the global pandemic on tourists' behaviour, the technique of ideas group development can be used, which is also practically implemented through the established forum of authorised employees of the tourism entity. Such a concept implies an individual presentation of proposals that a group of competent people comment on for a specific category of the new tourism product. A multidisciplinary approach is recommended (e.g. if it is a sports tourism product, kinesiologists, sports medicine doctors, former athletes, etc. are also competent). The lack of a technique for group development of ideas is the difference in the intensity of participation of individuals from different professions. The parallel use of *brainwriting* can compensate for the deficiency. When there is no personal confrontation of opinions, individuals are freer to express their views. The authors practise six methods of communication for evaluating potential ideas about new specialised tourism products:

(1) Collection and analysis of proposals for improving the basic characteristics of an each idea. After presenting the basic features, the discussants are free to express their opinions and propose improvements. Proposals are jointly analysed considering the possibility and costs of implementing such improvements, additional cost and contribution to the attractiveness of the new offer.
(2) Integrated tourism product platform – ideas are presented that complement each other and thus contribute to the impression of added value for each of them. The proposal of a new specialised tourism product is analysed as a component of the existing integrated offer platform.
(3) Proposing the improvement of the features of some of the existing ideas to create the impression of new content.
(4) Analysis of reversed assumptions – the assumptions that justify the attractiveness of the new offer in a specific category of specialised tourism products (sports, health, gastronomic, cultural and historical, etc.) are argued. Assumptions are analysed from the aspect of narrower interest segments of tourists, assuming their impressions regarding the different features of the proposed new contents.
(5) Proposing new content based on knowledge (conducted research and analysis) about the new tourist segment in the receptive or outgoing market. In direct communication with the representatives of that segment, one can learn what they would like to see in the offer.
(6) Mental mapping defines the most important categories within the specialised destination offer. The associations of the existing destination offer are analysed, and ideas about new tourism attractions are developed under these associations.

When evaluating and ranking ideas about new specialised tourism products, it is useful to analyse the complaints and suggestions of guests loyal to the destination. The comments of that segment of guests will point out shortcomings in the current offer, desirable modifications of existing contents, etc. When analysing ideas, there are practical e-forms on which considerations and evaluations are recorded according to criteria. Such criteria can include attractiveness for a certain segment of tourists, innovativeness/originality of the idea, ethical compliance with the standards of strategic emission markets, the competitiveness of the existing contents of the same category, segments of tourists possible to be attracted with new content, etc. The form and content categories of the e-form should be adapted to the ideas of the new content being analysed. Ultimately, the generalisation method predicts the possible satisfaction of tourists with each of the proposed ideas. Key competitive features are observed in relation to existing specialised contents of the same category. Based on all knowledge, recommended guidelines for developing promotion activities are observed. The weighted index method is also practical for evaluating each idea individually (Table 6).

The first column lists the key competitive features of the new tourism content. They are weighted according to their importance in the second column. In the third column, ratings are assigned to each element of each idea about a new specialised tourism product. The method of balancing the content of the integrated tourism offer is also used for the same purpose. The method argues for ranking different ideas considering their contribution to the overall destination offer (adapted from Lehman & Winner, 2005). When comparing similarly ranked ideas, the findings of the SWOT analysis of each of them are analysed.

A sample of selected ideas is further assessed to find those that will be easily commercialised and introduced into the destination offer. In their practice, the authors categorise the ideas of new specialised tourism products into:

a. Promising contents considering that they can attract the tourist's attention.
b. Side ideas, still potentially usable.
c. Ideas with content and features inferior to ideas classified under a) and b).

Ideas classified under c) are also recorded because they were selected based on specific arguments. They may be better classified in some new conditions in the tourist market. Ideas classified in a) are tested using the error of rejection and error of acceptance. The error of rejection occurs if some feature of a new specialised tourism product tends to be adapted exclusively to one, narrower tourist segment (for example, the content and concept of a gastronomic event should be adapted primarily to parents with children). Such an approach ignores the expectations of some other segments of tourists. An acceptance error occurs if the participants in the evaluation process of potential new content do not have similar competencies (among them, there are individuals whose competencies can be imposed on others). Ignoring the risk of rejection error and acceptance error can result in one of the following consequences:

Table 6. An Example of the Weighted Index Method in Evaluating New Product Ideas.

Conditions for Product Success	Relative Weight (a)	Point Score (b)	Product Rating (c = a × b)
Unique or pre-eminent product	0.40	0.8	0.32
High efficiency concerning the price	0.30	0.6	0.18
High dollar marketing support	0.20	0.7	0.14
Competition absence	0.10	0.5	0.05
Total	1.00		0.69

Source: Šerić (2018).

Note: Grading scale: 0.00–0.30 bad, 0.31–0.60 medium, 0.61–0.80 good. Minimal acceptance grade: 0.61.

(1) The new specialised tourism product will not achieve the desired sales.
(2) The cost of providing a new specialised tourism product will be higher than expected.
(3) The new specialised tourism product will achieve a lower profit margin than possible.

The consequences listed under 1) and 2) can be justified if the new tourism content contributes to the competitiveness of the destination offer (Šerić, Jakšić Stojanović, et al., 2023). In tourism practi`ce, there are examples of specialised tourism products that are an important component of the integrated destination offer. In this case, they are offered at subsidised prices (providers are compensated for the loss of earnings) or free of charge (Phillips & Louvieris, 2005; Sigala, 2004).

3.3. Concept Development

The concept development of a new specialised tourism product is carried out through related procedures that evaluate all potential characteristics to select the ones that are potentially more important to tourists. The concept of a new specialised tourism product is a list of basic features. The features are presented by emphasising what is entirely new and original and what contributes the most to the experience and added value of the offer. The form and characteristics of the new tourism content should be clearly presented, including the aspects that differentiate it from the current offers. For instance, the offer of a tourist stay at the lighthouses includes seclusion, landscape preservation, accommodation in buildings of cultural and historical heritage, etc. The concept of a new specialised tourism product will define the guidelines for the further development of the new tourism offer. One should highlight the strategically important features in the promotion. The concept should also provide answers on which characteristics it is possible to base the competitiveness of the new tourism content. If such argumentation is not possible at this stage, further business idea development should be completely abandoned. The difference between the idea and the conception of a potential new specialised tourism product is reflected in the complexity of the actual future content and the assessment of how attractive it can be to tourists. In the previous stages of developing a new specialised tourism product, judgements were made based on the opinions of individuals. At this stage, the opinions and attitudes of consulted tourism workers and tourists should be respected.

The concept is formed and tested in this phase of developing a new specialised tourism product. The testing is carried out in such a way as to simulate the possible reactions of tourists according to certain features of the new specialised tourism product. The procedure implies evaluating the new content from the point of view of tourists who will be offered the same. Simulations of possible reactions of tourists to new content are carried out by analysing secondary data on the experiences of other tourism stakeholders who commercialised new content from the same category of offer (sports, recreational, health, ethno-autochthonous, gastronomic and other categories of specialised tourism products). Analysing secondary data also reveals possible demand for the category of specialised products to which potential new content belongs. The final interpretation of findings is carried out through descriptive analysis of secondary data and content analysis (Šerić & Jurišić, 2014).

The concept assumes a clear vision of the subjective values of the new specialised tourism product for the targeted tourist segments. Concept testing (especially activities aimed at tourists) should also be used as publicity for future new tourism content. For the same purpose, it is possible to use communication (during concept testing) with representatives of the local tourist office. Reactions to publicity and the intensity of public response will be used to determine the form of future promotion of a new specialised tourism product.

Testing is carried out considering the following:

- Adaptation of the conception of new content to the needs and quality standards of the targeted tourist segments.
- Adaptation of the concept and identification with the needs of the target tourist segments.
- Comparative evaluation of the concept of new content with similar ones from the same category of specialised tourism products.
- Assessment of the elasticity of the concept concerning possibly necessary improvements and changes of individual features.
- Decision whether to continue developing a new specialised tourism product or to abandon it.

Concept testing can also be carried out by presenting the idea of new content to selected sales intermediaries. It is important to know how sales intermediaries perceive the value of new tourism content because they can be its essential promoters. Multimedia simulations (displays) are practical for this purpose. The focus should be on the vision of the integrity of the future offer, targeted tourist segments and strategic emitting tourism markets. At the same time, care should be taken regarding the clarity and persuasiveness of the offer. In direct communication with tourism workers and tourists, one verifies to what extent, in their opinion, the potential new content meets a specific tourist need. Testing the concept also determines the coverage of the tourist needs for which the new content is primarily intended. Concept testing will also indicate why the target tourist population would accept the new content.

Despite everything, concept testing is still often neglected in business practice (Šerić, Peronja, et al., 2020). The originality of the features of the new tourism offer is considered sufficient to attract the attention of tourists. Such thinking often results in poor sales of new content because tourists do not find it attractive. Concept testing of a new specialised tourism product is sometimes neglected to offer new content to tourists as soon as possible. The consequences can be even more devastating if the criteria for accepting the concept of a new tourism product have not been defined. After commercialisation, according to the BCG matrix, such a new tourism product will end up in the dog category or, at best, a question mark (Šerić, 2020). By neglecting the testing of the concept, wrong decisions are also possible in the promotion of new tourism content (Jakšić Stojanović & Šerić, 2018; Šerić, 2017, 2019b). Negative consequences can be multiplied in the development stages that follow. This increases the risk that the new specialised tourism product will not be adequately accepted on the market and will result in business losses. Authors researching this issue for tangible products warn of this risk (Aaker, 2001; Andersen et al., 1998; Churchill, 2002; Czinkota, 2000; Dibb et al., 2001; Lehman & Winner, 2005 and others). Unlike a tangible product, a tourism service is even more sensitive to misjudgements related to its characteristics. Testing one of several proposed concepts is even more critical if there is a dilemma in choosing them. Otherwise, the final selection will depend on individual judgements that may be contrary to the wishes and expectations of the target tourism clientele. A potential new specialised tourism product should be in harmony with a specific tourist need, and this harmony should be apparent. Another reason for testing the concept of a new specialised tourism product is the costs of its commercialisation (necessary logistics and others). Certain compromises may be needed due to the limited marketing budget of the tourism entity introducing new content to the tourism market.

The concept of a new specialised tourism product represents a concretised and elaborated market-oriented version of an idea that has been assessed as feasible and justified for continued development (Best, 2010; Šerić, 2016). The concept is based on the assumption that the target tourist segment will recognise the value of the new content and consider the price acceptable. Concerning the price issue, in this phase, the necessary level of quality of the provision of a new tourism service is determined. A presented concept of a new specialised tourism product will significantly simplify decision-making in the following development phases. Due to the above, it is not advisable to shorten the activity at this stage of developing a new specialised tourism product.

Chapter 4

Developing and Shaping the Marketing Strategy

4.1. Marketing Strategy and Implementation Tactics

If the presented concept is assessed as sustainable through testing, the marketing strategy's design is approached by considering all previous knowledge. The marketing strategy of the new specialised tourism content implies the planning of overall support for its commercialisation. As part of the strategy, other components of the marketing mix – price, distribution and promotion – are elaborated in more detail (Aaker, 2002; Anderson & Kerr, 2002). In this phase, simulations primarily related to the possible reactions of the target tourist segment according to specific tactics of the defined marketing strategy are also carried out. One should adapt the marketing strategy to the specifics of the new tourism content. It should be flexible (it is possible to modify it in the following development phases) to adapt, if necessary, to trends in the content category to which the new specialised tourism product belongs. The flexibility of the marketing strategy is also a prerequisite for its long-term applicability.

The marketing strategy is adapted to the targeted tourist segments and strategic emission markets with selected tactics (promotion, sales, etc.). At the same time, it is necessary to consider its influence on the image of the tourist entity that introduces new content to the market. The marketing strategy needs to be coordinated at the level of the total value chain of the new tourism content (provider of the new tourism service, a destination where it is provided, sales intermediaries and promotion of the same) (Moss & Atre, 2003). The strategy is designed based on knowledge from the previous stages of development. These findings (primary and secondary data) are classified according to the criteria of simulations used for this purpose (Brown, 2009; Šerić & Jurišić, 2014). The marketing strategy should assess the specifics of competitive relations in specialised tourism products, including new content (Šerić, Melović, et al., 2023).

The strategy is based on the existing relations of the receptive tourism market where the new content will be offered (tourist destination). It should be pointed out that the marketing strategy designed at this stage of development is a broader concept than a specialised tourism product strategy. The strategy of the

Specialised Tourism Products, 57–62
Copyright © 2024 Neven Šerić, Ivana Kursan Milaković and Ivan Peronja
Published under exclusive licence by Emerald Publishing Limited
doi:10.1108/978-1-83549-408-020241004

specialised tourism product is primarily focused on the features of the offered content. The marketing strategy is created by taking into account the specifics of the target tourist segment. Unlike a specialised tourism product, the marketing strategy also represents the fundamental basis of the commercialisation of new content, assuming the necessary logistics during the life cycle. The effectiveness of the marketing strategy of a new specialised tourism product implies planning, elaboration and implementation of tactics to implement it, as well as continuous monitoring and control of market reactions (Boyer et al., 2011; Doyle, 2002).

4.2. Marketing Strategy Development Plan

The marketing strategy development plan defines the activities of this phase (adapted from Lehman & Winner, 2005). The authors practise:

- Through simulation, determine the possible number of tourists interested in new tourism content during the primary tourism season, along with presenting the shopping habits of the target tourist segment, their demographic characteristics and other useable data. Based on sorted data, they suggest proposals for positioning new tourism content at the destination level (to increase visibility). Based on this simulation, the dynamics of return on investment in developing a new specialised tourism product can also be forecast.
- They argue the pricing strategy they have opted for and present individual prices and pricing policies. They link these data with the predicted sales and promotion model and the costs that these activities will generate (sales commissions, marketing budget, etc.).
- They justify the long-term business goals of introducing a new specialised tourism product into the offer with the simulation of income. They suggest the determinants for the long-term management of the elements of the marketing mix of a new specialised tourism product.

The marketing strategy should be as original as possible to further contribute to the differentiation of the new tourism content. It should connect the determinants of the strategy of the new tourism product so that the marketing strategy has a foothold in the characteristics of the new content (Cavalcanti, 2005). Suppose the new tourism content is not something completely new but rather the improvement or modification of an existing destination offer. In that case, developing the marketing strategy is advisable only partially. Based on experiences, the authors argue that the final shape of the marketing strategy for tourism offer that does not represent something completely new and innovative represents a significant differentiation lever, so it should be systematically and gradually developed. In implementing the marketing strategy of a new specialised tourism product, tactics are of particular importance, as they can be used to further enhance the added value of the new tourism content compared to other offers at the destination level. The marketing strategy also has the function of a preliminary analysis of the resolution of dilemmas that will arise in the development phases that follow. The marketing strategy of a new specialised tourism product should connect the identity of the basic content with the image of the tourist entity that will offer it, aiming to position the new content in the destination's offer.

Modifying the marketing strategy is carried out in the following stages of development, given new knowledge from the market environment, and primarily related to changes in the trends of the category of specialised tourism products to which the new content belongs. Modifications of the marketing strategy are also necessary for extraordinary situations, e.g. a decline in the purchasing power of the predominant tourist population in the destination, recessionary trends in the global tourism market and significant global disruptions such as the one caused by the COVID-19 pandemic. The consequences of assumed negative trends can be mitigated by proactive measures that are developed for this purpose as part of the marketing strategy, such as: shortening the time of providing the service for the sake of lower prices and introducing group arrangements for exclusively individual customers.

4.3. Development of Marketing Mix Elements

By defining the marketing strategy, one sets the starting points for the development of the elements of the marketing mix of the new specialised tourism product. The implementation of the marketing strategy is carried out by the tactics of managing the elements of the marketing mix. Furthermore, one decides on the final content characteristics of the potential new tourism offer, the required quality of the content, the creation of a different brand (or the introduction of new content under an existing brand) and others. The framework price strategy (presented in the previous development phase) is optimised in the context of the price. Following the specifics of the target tourist segment, individual pricing policies are developed. The price at which the new tourism content will be commercialised is determined by the breadth of the specialised tourism offer in the destination, relations between tourism stakeholders and the expected perception of what is offered to tourists.

Internal and external factors influence pricing decisions in tourism practice. Internal factors are the operating costs of the tourist entity, the expected sales model, sales goals, additional costs generated by introducing new tourism content and others. External factors are pricing strategies and pricing policies of competitors, legal regulations related to the category of a new specialised tourism product and rights to use the resources on which the new content is based. External factors include the attitudes and buying habits of the target tourist segment, existing relationships and changes in the target tourism markets, the impact of new technologies on the tourism economy and more.

The pricing policies chosen by the tourist entity will affect the intensity of demand for the new offer. In tourism practice, the price of a new offer is often determined according to the prices of similar ones in the same destination. One can also consider psychological pricing if the new tourism offer is entirely original. When choosing the price of a new specialised tourism product on a psychological basis, the basic features, quality of content, exclusivity and market availability of similar tourist offers are compared. Specific categories of specialised tourism products imply prestigiously high prices. These aspects refer to the rarity and value of the resources on which they are based, expensive and luxurious equipment that the provision of a new tourism service implies, the rarity of new tourism service and its inaccessibility to all interested tourists. The possible perception of everything that can contribute to the impression of added value in the mind of the target tourist is analysed. Accordingly, the possible upper price is determined. The upper psychological price limit is the maximum amount the target tourist segment is willing to pay for that category of specialised tourism product. If after commercialisation, the interest in the new tourism offer is not at the expected level, one can highlight a promotional price for a certain period of the year to encourage a trial (first) purchase and the creation of a spending habit. The promotional price is justified by the desire to acquaint the tourist population with new content. It is common to offer specific facilities at special prices (lower than regular prices) in periods outside the primary tourist season. One can also serve loyalty cards with an approved permanent discount for specific categories of tourists as an award for a certain number of purchases of a new specialised tourism product. After defining the basic pricing strategy, the selling price of the new tourism service is calculated based on one of three common methods (Lehman & Winner, 2005):

(1) price based on service costs,
(2) price based on supply and demand,
(3) price based on competition.

The cost-based price implies the amount spent on developing, selling and providing a new tourism service increased by the desired profit divided by the possible amount of individual services at the level of one or more tourism seasons. This approach to price calculation is justified if the tourist public's affirmative attitude is expected towards purchasing the offered new content. A prerequisite for an affirmative attitude towards buying is attractive and high-quality content that no one else offers in the destination. If there is no competition, it is possible to consider the return of all investments in developing a new specialised tourism product during one tourism season, given that the displayed selling price does not significantly influence the purchase.

The price based on the relationship between supply and demand implies consideration of everything offered by direct (offer of identical or similar tourist content) or indirect competition (total non-boarding offer) at the level of one destination. By looking at the existing destination offer, a decision is made about the reasonable price, regardless of the return period of the total investment. The price can ultimately be determined based on expected sales, to be lower than all similar offers in the destination or according to some other criterion with the condition that at least the minimum required monthly/annual sales are ensured. A higher price is determined in periods of intense demand (primary tourism season) and a slightly lower in periods outside the primary tourism season.

A price based on competition means setting a selling price close to similar or different non-boarding products that are a direct threat when making a potential purchase decision of a tourist. The final price is determined below, above or at the level of the prices of the content and quality of service of similar tourism products. A lower price than competitors' prices is desirable if they keep similar prices throughout the year. In the primary tourist season, there is no need for a lower price than the prices of competitors who offer identical attractive tourism facilities in terms of content and quality. A price above the level of competitors' prices is practised if the new specialised tourism product is superior in features, quality and service to everything else that is offered in the destination.

Regardless of the concept that will be chosen for calculating the price of a new specialised tourism product, one should also consider the possible reactions of tourists to different approaches. The tourist analyses the new offer from the aspect of originality, experience, attractiveness, exclusivity and added value for what is paid. The price determined in the phase of commercialisation of the new tourism content can be adjusted to a higher one without consequences for the sale if it is about simpler tourist services of lower value. Raising the price can result in negative publicity and the loss of existing customers if it is about more complex tourism services, especially those that can be classified as luxury. The findings of many authors' studies have proven that the same tourism clientele would accept a higher price without question than the one that was determined at the beginning of commercialisation of a new specialised tourism product. However, the formation of the same price by increasing the price when introducing a new offer generates negative reactions from tourists (giving up future purchases, dissatisfaction, etc.).

Tourists can perceive price reductions of a new specialised tourism product in the maturity phase as the beginning of the withdrawal of the offer from the market, which encourages additional purchases. It is important to logically justify any reduction in the prices of tourism services so as not to create the impression of a reduction in quality. Explanations based on loyalty to a tourism destination or tourism subject to a specific service provider are also practical. One should also monitor competitors' reactions together with their long-term business interests (Ambler, 2000; Šerić, 2009b).

Promotional activities for a new specialised tourism product are developed following the goals related to the planned return on investment and the goals of marketing communication. Activities are designed separately for each stage of the life cycle of a new specialised tourism product (internet promotion, publicity on receptive and target emission markets, economic propaganda on selected emission markets, sales promotion activities, direct marketing on target emission markets and public relations on receptive and target emission markets prevail). The growth of the potential of sales via the internet, the sales opportunities provided by social networks and the significantly lower costs of promotional activities are increasingly directing them into the virtual sphere. The tourist public trusts publicity more than other forms of promotion, so it is advisable to maintain it throughout the entire life cycle of a specialised tourism product. It is advisable to practise economic propaganda on the target emitting tourist markets immediately before commercialising and introducing a new specialised tourism product. The focus should be on the fundamental characteristics of the new content, which also argue for added value. Economic propaganda tactics are implemented through *pioneering*, *competitive*, *comparative* or *cooperative* concepts. Pioneering economic propaganda is focused on stimulating interest in the new content and is effective for innovative content. Competitive economic propaganda promotes interest in a trial purchase and is recommended under various specialised tourism products' competition conditions. Comparative economic propaganda is based on emphasising differences concerning competitive offers. Cooperative economic propaganda is based on the joint promotional activities of tourism stakeholders who participate in creating, selling and providing specialised tourism services.

Economic propaganda also serves to remind the tourist public about a specific specialised tourism offer and the entity that offers it. Activities to promote the sale of a new specialised tourism product are practised in the phase of its introduction to the tourist market. In the budget of the marketing strategy, it is advisable to allocate funds for this purpose. They are implemented with additional incentives for sales agents and tourists (discounts for group bookings, for multiple weekly and monthly purchases, etc.). Personal selling can represent a vital purchase incentive for specialised tourism products throughout the life cycle. One can more appropriately present complex (intricate content, multiple related services) and luxury specialised tourism products through direct contact with potentially interested tourists. Direct marketing implies an interactive approach to tourists with continuous personal communication. The sale of a new specialised tourism product can be realised through an already established system (separate sales point, hotel receptions and travel agencies), while an exclusive and special sales system can also be established. Such a sales model contributes to the impression of the added value of new content. Sales efficiency and implementation in relation to the plan should be continuously monitored, new models developed and existing ones modified accordingly.

Chapter 5

Business Analysis and Marketing Test of a New Specialised Tourism Product

5.1. Analysis of Attractiveness and Profitability

Attractiveness and cost-effectiveness analysis is carried out in order to demonstrate the commercialisation potential of the new tourist content. Simulations are carried out based on the final concept of a new specialised tourism product. The interest of specific tourist segments and potential sales of new tourist content during and outside the peak tourist season will be evaluated. In the earlier stages of development, the previous investments and costs of commercialisation (and provision) of a new tourist offer have been estimated, and based on simulations of possible sales, the profitability of commercialisation and the dynamics of return on investment are known. The results of the analysis reveal correctable and possibly irreparable errors in the design and characteristics of the new specialised tourism product. Irreparable errors include the assumption that further development and marketing of new content will be foregone even though it has not yet been fully developed.

The characteristics of the potential new specialised tourism product and the assumed quality of the service should be harmonised with the standards of the target outbound tourist markets, i.e. the strategic tourism segment (dominant customers).

The modification of individual features and additional improvement of the new tourist offer is carried out only after the completion of this phase of development and on the basis of the identified correctable mistakes. Correctable mistakes can be compensated by price and pricing policy and by the way new tourist services are offered. The final adjustment is made when the final prototype of the new tourist service is developed. The estimate of revenue from the sale of a new specialised tourism product is calculated based on an assessment of the intensity of the need for potential new thematic content and expected interest considering the content and price. At this stage of development, the attractiveness of the new tourist content is assessed from the perspective of the typical destination tourist. Information about the structure of visitors to the destination where the new content will be offered is useful. The analysis includes all variables that have a

Specialised Tourism Products, 63–77

Copyright © 2024 Neven Šerić, Ivana Kursan Milaković and Ivan Peronja
Published under exclusive licence by Emerald Publishing Limited
doi:10.1108/978-1-83549-408-020241005

significant impact on the initial purchase decision (the first purchase of a new tourist service). The habits of potential customers, typical and specific (for specialised tourism products of the same category) purchasing behaviour and quality standards for a particular category of tourist offer are analysed. The availability of active, technical and financial resources for the continuity of the provision of the new tourist service is also assessed. The financial investment required to maintain the quality of the infrastructure that supports the provision of the new tourism service as well as the promotional efforts required are estimated. Simulations are used to evaluate the effectiveness of each promotional activity (marketing metrics). Based on the simulations, the budget for the planned activities for the future marketing of the new tourist content is proposed.

The authors analyse the tourists' interest and potential revenue from a new specialised tourism product by estimating the annual/seasonal sales of this content, taking into account the existing structure of non-board sales of the destination and the average non-board consumption per tourist. Statistical data from the previous tourist season and other useful secondary data are used in the calculation (e.g. habits of typical visitors to the destination, planned promotional activities, etc.). Such an estimate is corrected taking into account available and planned new distribution channels. It is necessary to take into account the different reactions of tourists' age segments and, in accordance with this structure of tourists, the adaptation of new content to global trends. Following their own research (Šerić, 2017, 2019b; Šerić & Batalić, 2018; Šerić & Marušić, 2019; Šerić, Mihanović, et al., 2020), while accounting for the recent generation age span insights (Beresford, 2023), the authors found differences among the generational cohorts:

- *Traditionalists* (over 77 years old prefer conservative and simpler tourist attractions).
- *Baby Boomers* (aged 59–77, they are positive towards all new tourist facilities and represent the largest share of non-board consumption at the destination level).
- *Generation X* (aged 43–58, they prefer functional tourist attractions with ecological features and clear added value).
- *Generation Y* (aged 27–42, important promotion of new tourist content through social networks, preference for tourist consumption in groups).
- *Generation Z* (born after the year of 1997, i.e. aged 11–26, promotion of new tourist content mainly through digital media).

It is also worth mentioning Generation Alpha (young children up to 7 years), who will grow up in a specific environment threatened by various pollutants and will therefore show a particular interest in specialised health tourism offers (Jakšić Stojanović et al., 2019b; Jakšić Stojanović, Janković, Šerić, & Vukilić, 2019).

In the analysis, it is advisable to focus on the specifics of the particular target market that is of strategic importance for the tourism destination (Hedin et al., 2011; Jakšić Stojanović et al., 2019a; Šerić & Marušić, 2019; Šerić, Mihanović, et al., 2020; Šerić, Peronja, et al., 2020). At the same time, special attention should be paid to adapting the quality of specific content to the standards and expectations of the target tourism segments. The specific characteristics of the new specialised tourism market are analysed according to their attractiveness for penetrating, serving or limiting parts of the strategic outbound markets (Šerić & Jurišić, 2014, 2015). Each of these parts implies a different promotion of new target content (Baggio, 2020; Boes et al., 2016; Buhalis & Sinarta, 2019). The penetrating part of a target market consists of tourists who frequently test new tourist content. The serviceable part (early majority and part of the late majority – Šerić, 2016) consists of the tourist population open to new experiences, likely to test new tourist content during their stay in the destination, but they need to be made aware of it. Repeated purchases, i.e. tourists' overall expressed interest in new content, also depend on the breadth and depth of all tourism content in the destination. A limited part of the target market consists of half of the late majority and the undecided (Šerić, 2016). These tourists may not opt for new content during their stay in the destination if the price is not particularly attractive (low considering the impression of added value), and the cause may also lie in their prevailing non-board consumption buying habits (when and where they spend).

In the analysis, the available part of the tourist population includes the tourists who statistically stay in the destination during certain periods of the main and other parts of the season. From the total number, nationalities that are not positive towards new experiences or have lower non-board consumption during their stay in the destination should be excluded.

The potential part of the tourist population includes tourists who stay in the destination for a certain period of time and belong to the segment of wealthier guests in terms of accommodation and non-boarding consumption (Šerić & Jurišić, 2014).

In parallel with the classification of the tourist population that has stayed in the destination where the new content is marketed in the past years, the different experiences of non-boarding consumption at the destination level are also analysed. Special attention should be paid to the prevailing pricing strategy and pricing policy for the sale of existing specialised tourism content, as well as the promotional efforts for that content. It is also useful to learn about the perceptions of numerous tourist segments regarding existing specialised tourism content in the destination's offerings. Particularly, valuable data and information can be used to clarify dilemmas about the characteristics and appropriate price of new content (Kumar, 2005).

Based on all these findings, the appropriate price, quality and promotion of the new tourism service is determined. The solution of the dilemma is supported by market experiences with existing specialised tourism products. Is the new tourism service more attractive, better quality, more attractively priced, more accessible, safer than the existing competing non-board facilities? Based on the answers to these and other questions listed in this chapter, the dilemmas and doubts that will arise in the remaining stages of the development of a new specialised tourism product will be resolved.

If the tourism facility developing a new specialised tourism product successfully promotes and sells other non-board facilities through selected sales agents, their thoughts on the sales volume of the new facilities will be included in the analysis.

The spatial scope of sales should also be noted, that is, the necessary promotional activities that would attract tourists from other destinations in the region without facilities similar to the new specialised tourism product.

The analysis concludes with an assessment of the short-, medium- and long-term volume of potential new content sales. The total amount of individual purchases that may be realised during the analysed periods is considered, taking into account the day/night periods when such a category of non-board content is typically purchased. Given the growing intensity of climate change over the last decade, this should also be taken into account (hydrometeorological deterioration, deviations from normal temperatures and number of sunny days per month, etc.).

The estimate of the cost of selling/providing a new specialised tourist service includes all fixed and variable components of the calculation. The structure of fixed costs should include the costs incurred during the development of a new specialised tourist offer. Does the new specialised tourist service incur extraordinary preventive costs due to higher safety standards for tourists (e.g. paramedics, specialised tour guides, etc.)? Variable costs are calculated as a direct result of the process of providing a new tourist service, taking into account promotional discounts/discounts for tourists and sales agents.

The assessment of potential revenues from the marketing of a new specialised tourism product depends on prices and pricing policies. At all stages of the development of a new specialised tourism product, the reasons for the decision and the profit targets set should be kept in mind. Knowing these reasons and objectives will also help clarify dilemmas. Valuable are also all the findings that can show the elasticity of tourist demand depending on the category of the specialised tourist offer that includes new content. Based on all these facts, it is possible to evaluate the long-term financial viability of the new tourist content during its expected life cycle.

5.2. Market Feasibility Analysis

The findings from the analysis of the attractiveness and profitability of a new specialised tourism product form the basis for the evaluation of the market feasibility of the new offer. The results indicate how many years it is possible to maintain satisfactory tourist interest in the new offer. Marketability depends on the complexity of the offer, the cost of maintaining the necessary infrastructure and the legal regulations related to the resources on which the specialised tourism product is based.

The determinants of the chosen marketing strategy (Chapter 4) and the necessary lifespan should also be evaluated at this stage of the development of a new specialised tourism product. The lifetime of the new offer should allow the depreciation of all development costs with an acceptable annual profit. The calculation is based on determining the potential daily revenue from the provision of new tourist offer on the estimated number of days per year. The number of days per year, that new content sales are counted, represents the annual average of sunny days without strong winds or extreme heat. The number of such days is multiplied by the estimated maximum daily sales of the new offer (based on the simulated price – see Chapter 4.3). The maximum daily sales also depend on the average number of guests in the destination or the share of the target segment. For this calculation, statistical reports of the local tourist office on the number and structure of guests in the destination in previous years are used (Cvetkoska & Barišić, 2014).

These results provide information about the possible and desirable return dynamics of the investment in the development of a new specialised tourism product.

Depending on the calculated indicators, it is suggested which correctable errors of the existing concept of the new specialised tourism product should still be eliminated (additional modifications of the individual characteristics of the offer, the estimated price, the duration of the provision of the new tourism service, etc.). Additional modifications are used to simulate the long-term sustainability of the new offer (Dibb et al., 2001).

The identification of one or more irreparable errors qualifies the new content as unsustainable, which would mean that the idea should definitely be abandoned. Irreparable errors are the finding that the number of days with satisfactory hydrometeorological conditions in the destination does not ensure the desirable/ necessary return on investment, that the projected/simulated price of the new offer does not ensure a satisfactory annual net profit (remaining after calculating the depreciation of the funds spent on development and the costs of providing new tourist services, etc.). An exception to this rule is new tourist facilities classified by the local self-government unit as strategic (significant contribution to strengthening the attractiveness and visibility of the destination in the global tourism market). For such tourist facilities, co-financing is possible at the destination level, so this amount should also be included in the return on investment (Šerić, 2018; Šerić, Jakšić Stojanović, et al., 2023).

The marketability of the new specialised tourist offer depends on the estimated intensity of interest and purchase by tourists. The intensity of demand and consumption of a new offer will be satisfactory if it is positioned in a niche that ensures good visibility and competitiveness (Šerić & Jurišić, 2014). Sustainability depends to a significant extent on the number of visitors to the destination from strategic segment of potential consumers of new offer (Dolnicar, 2019). For this calculation, in addition to the statistical reports of previous years, the proportion of those who can be assumed to pay an acceptable price for the new content should be included, based on the proportion of the destination's non-board revenue. On the other hand, the calculation should also include indicators of growth/decrease in annual visits to the

Table 7. Adventure Activities – Descriptive Data.

Statement	Mean	St.dev
4.1. Adventure activities help me to escape my everyday life.	4.87	0.35
4.2. Adventure activities help me avoid boredom.	5.00	0.00
4.3. Adventure activities bring novelty in my life.	4.37	0.74
4.4. I like the thrill of an adventure.	5.00	0.00
4.5. I like the rush that adventures bring.	3.50	0.75
4.6. I like the danger associated with an adventure.	2.37	1.06
4.7. Adventure activities help me develop my skills, i.e. competence.	4.12	1.45
4.8. I like to experience new things.	4.75	0.70
4.9. I am a person oriented towards sensation-seeking.	3.62	1.51
4.10. I see adventure activities as self-fulfilling.	3.75	1.58
4.11. I like variety-seeking.	3.75	1.16
4.12. Adventure activities are important to me for my personal growth.	3.62	1.51
4.13. Adventure activities are important to me for my self-discovery.	4.37	0.91
4.14. Adventure activities are important to me for my self-expression.	3.37	1.18
4.15. I like the risk associated with the adventure activities.	2.25	1.03
4.16. I like the adrenalin that adventure offers.	4.50	0.53
4.17. I feel pleasure and joy when engaged in adventure activities.	4.75	0.46
4.18. Adventure activities are fun.	4.75	0.46
4.19. I feel happy when engaged in adventure activity.	4.62	0.51
4.20. I like the challenge that adventure activities offer.	4.75	0.46
4.21. I believe I achieve self-actualisation through adventures.	3.87	0.99
4.22. I like the social contacts acquired through adventure activities.	4.50	0.75
4.23. The risk of my adventure activity is worth the reward that I obtain from it.	3.25	1.03
4.24. I think I am born for adventures.	3.75	1.03
4.25. I have a passion for adventures.	4.12	0.83
4.26. Adventure activities make me feel empowered.	4.12	0.83
4.27. I reward myself through adventure activities.	4.00	0.75
4.28. Adventure activities give me freedom.	4.25	0.88

Table 7. *(Continued)*

Statement	Mean	St.dev
4.29. Adventure activity represents who I am.	3.62	0.91
4.30. Adventure activity offers a status.	2.37	1.40
4.31. Adventure activities regenerate my spirit.	4.25	0.88
4.32. Adventure activities are important for my well-being.	3.25	1.03
4.33. I can enjoy authenticity and unique offers through adventures.	4.37	0.74
4.34. I like the natural resources that adventure activities include.	4.87	0.35
4.35. I find destinations associated with my adventure activities attractive.	4.87	0.35
4.36. I like exploring different cultures through my adventure activities.	4.62	0.74
4.37. I like the contact with nature that my adventure activity offers.	4.75	0.46
4.38. Concerning adventure activities, convenience of facilities is crucial.	3.75	0.88
4.39. When in an adventure, accessibility of transportation is important to me.	3.25	1.03

Source: Research.

destination by the strategic guest segment (Butler, 2020). The strategic guest segment includes the percentage of those tourists for whom the new tourism offer is primarily suitable in terms of features and price. If there is a risk of a decline in tourist visits to the destination (recessionary trends in the strategically outbound tourist markets, hotspots of crisis and war in the surrounding areas, the possibility of an increase in the number of patients suffering from the COVID-19 pandemic in the receptive/strategic outbound tourist market, according to Girish, 2020 and the like), this should be included in the final calculation of the evaluation of the feasibility of a new specialised tourism product.

For new tourism products that are not technically or financially complex in terms of cost or performance (providing services), the business risks are significantly lower (Cooper, 2021), especially if the expected unit price of the new tourism service is low. The only thing that needs to be taken into account is the required average number of visitors to the destination per year. The key data for assessing the sustainability of new offer are the average number of potential customers per day in the total mass of visitors to the destination in the period when it is technically possible to provide a particular service (hydrometeorological conditions).

New specialised tourism products that reach the maturity stage of demand/sales during the first year of marketing often have a shorter lifespan (Buhalis et al., 2019; Prorok et al., 2019; Šerić, 2016; Šerić, Peronja, et al., 2020). Maintaining satisfactory demand for a specialised tourism product during the maturity stage depends on maintaining the interest of the target clientele. Maintaining the interest of the tourist (and local) target clientele depends on the marketing creativity of the entity that provides the tourist service (Pearce et al., 2003; Šerić, Dadić, et al., 2020; Šerić, Kalinić, et al., 2011; Sigala, 2004). In their own practice, the authors implement this by modifying the content and characteristics of the offer and by changing the personnel providing the tourist service (Jakšić Stojanović & Šerić, 2019b; Jakšić Stojanović et al., 2020; Jakšić Stojanović, Šerić, et al., 2019; Šerić, 2019b; Šerić & Marušić, 2019; Šerić, Jakšić Stojanović, et al., 2023).

If a new specialised tourism product shows a high rate of repeated purchases (the same customers choose it frequently), it means that its characteristics and price are adequately adapted to the target segment of tourists. By analysing additional characteristics of this segment of tourists (motives, value attitudes, etc.), it is possible to ensure their long-term loyalty (Lehman & Winner, 2005; Peter & Donnelly, 2004; Pivčević et al., 2016; Ries & Trout, 2001; Šerić & Jurišić, 2014). For specialised tourism products whose sales structure (frequently repeated purchases by the same customers) indicates a high degree of adaptation to the desires of the target segment, it is not recommended to significantly change the price or content (Jafari & Xiao, 2021; Lidwell et al., 2006; Lockwood, 2009; Šerić, Jurišić, et al., 2015; Šerić, Jakšić Stojanović, et al., 2023; Šerić, Peronja, et al., 2020).

It is recommended that the marketability of a new specialised tourism product be analysed by a person responsible for controlling or by a person from the top management level in the case of large. This analysis implies broader, strategic considerations of the company as a whole, in contrast to the usual corporate analyses in the tourism industry, which are carried out by employees of the finance or research and development departments.

The final decision on whether to continue development or abandon the idea of a new specialised tourism product based on the results of the profitability analysis is made exclusively at the level of the top management/owner of the business. It should be kept in mind that unilateral conclusions, regardless of the experience of, always represent a risk, as certain facts may not be recognised that, despite the results of this analysis, may have a positive/negative impact on the marketing and sale of a new tourism service (Šerić & Luković, 2013; Šerić & Meža, 2014; Šerić, et al., 2012, 2014; Šerić, Pavlinović, et al., 2011).

In addition, the assessment of the marketability of a new specialised tourism product includes an analysis of the break-even point, i.e. the period required to cover all the costs of developing and marketing new content. By linking this estimate to the average duration of service per unit purchased and the number of days per year that there will be interested tourists, the analysis of market feasibility is completed. In practice, the authors present the analysis of the sustainability of the new specialised tourism product as optimistic, pessimistic and the most probable variant. These statements are the result of differently evaluated risk impacts (ordinary, special and extraordinary business risks – Aaker, 2001;

Ambler, 2000; Baker & Riley, 1994; Barros & Alves, 2004; Brown, 2009). The special variables that are taken into account in the optimistic and pessimistic variants of the market feasibility analysis are indexed according to the state of the global and receptive tourism market (Andersen & Petersen, 1993; Coasta, 2020; Martín et al., 2015; Meyers et al., 2006; Soysal-Kurt, 2017).

5.3. Test Marketing

Test marketing of a special tourism product can be practically carried out using the experimental method by offering part or all of the new content to a small number of selected tourists (Šerić & Jurišić, 2014). If sufficient logistical support for the provision of new offer has not yet been organised (not all have been installed on the new climbing route), the experiment can be conducted virtually. The virtual experiment is conducted with a computer presentation. Test marketing in a virtual environment allows for the inclusion of a broader tourist population, i.e. those tourists who are not in the destination where the new content is offered during the test marketing period (Baars et al., 2008). Simulation or virtual testing is practical because of its simplicity, speed and lower cost. An experiment realises higher costs, especially for the hired personnel (guides, companions, instructors).

The reactions of the people selected for test marketing result from their perceptions of and experiences with the new tourist offer. An experiment in a real environment, in contrast to a computer simulation, shows more realistically the reaction of an individual exposed to the experiment. For this reason, the findings of virtual test marketing should be understood relatively because the tourist expresses a real reaction to new content exclusively in a real, natural environment based on experience.

However, virtual test marketing is increasingly being practised in the development of new specialised tourism products because it allows for low cost, complete safety of the people included in the test and also broader coverage of tourists in the sample. The results of virtual test marketing are used in the analysis of the characteristics of the new tourist offer in the perception of tourists. Such test marketing is suitable for simpler specialised tourism products and for any content that is more important than the environment in which it is offered (e.g. a mobile water park for children that can be placed anywhere by anchoring it to the ground).

For new specialised tourist facilities where the ambience is of particular importance to the overall experience, it is recommended to conduct test marketing in the real environment (tourist stay in the lighthouse). Test marketing in a real environment is recommended for increasingly complex specialised tourism products, the development of which involves significant investments.

Test marketing in the real environment should encourage respondents to personally question their willingness to choose a new offer. Based on their responses, impressions about the various features of the offer can be analysed.

These findings are relevant to decisions about modifying, improving or simplifying the content of the offer.

When conducting virtual test marketing, the content of the offer should be presented as completely and authentically as possible. The added value of the new tourist offer should be particularly emphasised (following Aaker et al., 1992). For more complex, specialised tourism products, authors practise the implementation of virtual test marketing in two phases (Šerić, 2008, 2009a, 2014, 2018; Šerić, Kalinić, et al., 2011; Šerić & Luković, 2010, 2013; Šerić, Mihanović, et al., 2020; Šerić & Perišić, 2012). The first one is conducted as a pre-market test, i.e. the tourist target group is familiarised with the main features of the new content (Jakšić Stojanović & Šerić, 2019a). It is useful to repeat the pre-market test immediately before the start of sales of a new specialised tourism product. So far, all important dilemmas have been solved, so this test has primarily a promotional function (Andersen et al., 1998; Anderson & Kerr, 2002). Based on the results, all remaining doubts can be resolved and the cost of logistical support for the provision of a new specialised tourism service can be simplified and reduced (following Šerić, Dadić, et al., 2020; Šerić & Luetić, 2016).

The second phase of test marketing involves a full presentation of the new content. People who have not shown significant interest in the presented new tourist content during the pre-market test are excluded from the test. The full presentation is conducted to finalise the content and features of the specialised tourism service. The insights gained by implementing test marketing in practice lead to a higher profit margin (Šerić, Vitner Marković, et al., 2017).

Conventional test marketing can also be carried out. Tourism companies carry it out of selected tourism fairs, where they promote the new specialised tourist service to selected sales intermediaries, i.e. agents in this target market (Šerić, 2004). Also practical are presentations of new tourist content in the context of the presentation of integration destination offers, in the context of which the same is offered (Richards, 2019). *ID RIVA tours* represents many of the specialised tourism products of the Republic of Croatia in the strategically important target market of Germany. This sales agent not only knows the expectations and desires of Germans very well but has also always shown exceptional sensibility for new tourist content (Šerić, 2004). Such agents are the optimal solution for conducting conventional test marketing at tourism fairs.

The continuity of conventional test marketing at tourism fairs strengthens the attractiveness and competitiveness of a receptive tourism country (Šerić, 2011; Šerić & Talijančić, 2011). One gets the impression that the national tourist offer is constantly being supplemented and improved. Moreover, new content is promoted, and potential tourists are encouraged to choose it. In some cases, the originality and attractiveness of the new specialised tourist offer contribute to the choice of a particular destination (Šerić, 2012a, 2012b). For this reason, conventional test marketing implies the use of various marketing tools. They are in accordance with the prepared marketing scenario (Šerić & Uglešić, 2014).

Regardless of the way in which test marketing is carried out, its weaknesses should also be taken into account:

- Test marketing assumes an additional cost in the process of developing a new specialised tourism product.
- There is always a dilemma regarding the appropriate way to conduct it.
- Conducting test marketing requires planning and time for implementation, which prolongs the process of developing a new specialised tourism product.
- Conducting test marketing draws the public's attention to the new tourism product and thus to potential competitors in the same or surrounding destinations offering something similar.

Despite the weaknesses mentioned above, test marketing is recommended and desirable when developing a new specialty tourism product. This is especially true for more complex and logistically costly new tourism offerings. The weaknesses of test marketing are reduced to an acceptable level through planning and an adapted implementation scenario, in particular, through the choice of method, location and partners in the implementation of test marketing.

5.4. Psychology of Tourists

Adventure tourism has grown exponentially and received much attention recently due to its ability to create unique sensations (Nasution et al., 2023). It encompasses trips to gain new experiences while often involving risk and a certain extent of danger (Tschapka, 2006). Adrenalin tourism is also used as a term and represents adventure tourism's sub-category (CBI, 2023). It is one of the biggest tourism niches and is expected to increase (CBI, 2023). Such activities usually include interactions with the natural environment, whereas the outcome depends on the individual, place and organisation of the tourism experience (Tschapka, 2006). Participating in extreme tourist activities is a profoundly personal decision, including the risks and rewards (Baruah, 2023). The level of experience in an activity, i.e. one's familiarity with adventure activity, is also essential since it affects not only the motivations of an individual but also the risk-taking behaviour (Tschapka, 2006).

5.4.1. Individual's Motivation

Consumer motivation is vital for choosing products or services, i.e. decision-making (Schiffman et al., 2012), and tourism is no excuse. In a tourism context, motivation refers to reasons, i.e. motives, why people travel and/or consume tourism content. Adventure means different things to consumers, i.e. tourists; therefore, it is subjective and poses a challenge for the companies and providers in adventure tourism (Koskinen & Öhberg, 2014). Studies suggest that genetic, environmental and personal factors influence people engaging in risky activities, whereas some people are born with a taste for adventure (McMillan Manley, 2016). Much emphasis is put on the personality and emotions. For instance, personality is thought to be a vital factor (Koskinen & Öhberg, 2014) because it denotes one's openness and proneness for adventures. Scholars indicate that a personality is an internal mix of environmental and genetic factors (McMillan Manley, 2016). Some claim that different factors play a role, while sensation-seeking personality might be crucial (Kancheva, 2017). Moreover, emotions stimulate motivation (Koskinen & Öhberg, 2014), which might explain why someone is motivated to engage in adventure activities and experiences and what drives them. Some studies claim that people who have difficulties experiencing and expressing emotions might be more prone to risk-taking activities, thus perceiving the adventures as a path towards empowerment and rewarding themselves (McMillan Manley, 2016). Hence, tourists might engage in adventure tourism for many reasons. The most common reason is escapism; that is, they want to escape their everyday sceneries, whereas for such activities, physical and mental challenges play an essential role, and participation from the tourists is required (Tschapka, 2006). Researchers argue that adventure tourists are a diverse group, i.e. motivated by different motives, whereas experience, age and gender also play essential roles in affecting their motives and motivation (Pomfret & Bramwell, 2016).

5.4.2. Push and Pull Motivations

Studies suggest that tourists are motivated by inner motives (e.g. push factors), such as boredom in their lives, business, need for relaxation, health problems (Mansfeld, 1992) or thrill-seeking (McMillan Manley, 2016). Therefore, push factors refer to the intrinsic motivations of an individual, i.e. drivers of seeking specific tourism experiences, whereas novelty might be seen as the main driver, followed by enjoying nature, environmental education, escapism and thrill (Giddy, 2018). The least attractive motivators in Giddy's (2018) study were found to be skills development, risk and socialisation, which is sort of contradictory to the vast body of literature. Namely, Gürer and Kural (2023) determined the vital role of socialisation and spiritual regeneration for adventure sports (e.g. climbing), while other intrinsic motivations were also established, such as happiness and fun. On the other side, adventure seekers might be well-prepared, careful and intelligent athletes with excellent knowledge of nature and the environment (McMillan Manley, 2016). In addition, researchers (Koskinen & Öhberg, 2014) add sensation-seeking and physiological involvement to pull factors. Others see adventure tourism as enjoying authenticity, localised experiences, unique characteristics and offers (Modiano, 2011). Giddy (2018) argues that the increased growth and commercialisation of adventure tourism drive changes in the profile of the individuals who engage in adventure tourism activities. Namely, many factors influence decision-making, while the motivation for engaging in such activities differs. Most studies focused on risk-seeking motives; however, recent studies reveal that it is not all about the actual risk but rather the perception of risk manifested as thrill and rush (Akbar, 2017; Giddy, 2018). Furthermore, researchers argue that the rush, rather than a risk, enables the attraction concerning adventure tourism activities (Buckley, 2020). Scholars indicate that individuals can gain well-being while engaging in risky and/or adventure activities due to acquiring positive feelings, such as happiness (Holm et al., 2017). Besides this, self-actualisation is a crucial driver. Namely, tourists might strive to achieve self-actualisation through searching for specific settings, i.e. adventures (Tschapka, 2006).

Concerning adventure tourism, the environment, i.e. pull factors, also plays an essential role, such as the natural resources and attractiveness of the destination (Foo & Rosetto, 1998). Studies indicate that both intrinsic (push) and extrinsic (pull) factors should be assessed when dealing with consumer/tourist motivations (Uysal & Jurowski, 1994). Based on Uysal and Jurowski's (1994) push and pull approach, the main push factors are family togetherness, appreciation of natural resources, escape from everyday routine and adventure and building relationships (Giddy, 2018). In contrast, pull factors encompass essential tourist resources, information and convenience of facilities and accessibility and transportation (Giddy, 2018). Furthermore, according to Martin and Priest (1986), the reasons for adventure experience should be sought in balancing the components of risk and competence. In addition, Tschapka (2006) indicates that the reasons for adventure tourism are the need for challenge, self-fulfilment, social interaction and personal development. Adventure tourism and motivators mainly centre on risk, danger and adrenaline, while tourists experience new reality through achievements of freedom, identity and status (Kane & Tucker, 2004).

5.4.3. Empirical Research

For profiling, i.e. disclosing the motives of tourists prone to risk and adventure, we conducted structured interviews with several individuals prone to risk and adrenalin activities. The structured interview included seven open-ended questions supplemented with one closed question (five-point Likert scale) with multiple items about intrinsic and extrinsic motives that were formulated based on the relevant literature. The interview also included demographic data such as age, gender, education and job position. The respondents were from Croatia, whereas the interview occurred in November 2023. All respondents were told that there were no right or wrong answers, and that all responses were anonymous while participation was voluntary.

The main research question was: *What are the primary motivations for adventure and risk-prone tourists concerning specialised tourism products?*

Result's Analysis

Eight individuals, five women and three men, participated in separate interviews. Age ranged from 21 to 51 years old for women and 29 to 40 for men. All interviewees had higher education degrees. Their job positions included professor position, journalist, hotel director, owner of tourist agency, owner of businesses for tourism and hospitality and hotel marketing manager position.

Q1) Which adventure activities do you prefer and enjoy?

Concerning adventure activities, the research results show that respondents prefer and enjoy the following activities: high mountain and inaccessible terrain climbing, free-climbing, buggy and quad drives, fast river rafting, scuba diving, cycling, kayaking, paddle surfing, solo travelling, skiing, snowmobile driving, adrenalin parks (suspension bridges and nets), zip lining, ballooning, electric foil boarding and paragliding.

Q2) Which adventure activities do you have the most experience with? What is the extent of such experience?

The respondents have the most experience with scuba diving (some more than 20 years of experience), skiing and climbing, solo travelling, cycling, kayaking, hiking and rafting.

Q3) Why do you engage in your favourite adventure activities? What are your main reasons and motives?

Respondents believe each adventure activity represents the opportunity to reveal new life aspects while offering unique and enriching experiences. Some indicate that such activities evoke high levels of adrenalin and curiosity, which drives them even more to these activities. They claim that such activities offer the possibility for personal growth. Precisely, they disclose the main motives for adventure activities as the following: adrenalin feeling, excitement, curiosity, the desire to explore, testing own limits and stamina, carelessness, everyday life escape, revealing new dimensions, active vacation, nature connection and intimacy, variety of experiences, intensity of experience, unrestrainedness, controlled adventure, relaxation.

Q4) Concerning your favourite adventure activities, please indicate how do you feel about the following statements? (1 – strongly disagree, 2 – disagree, 3 – neither disagree or agree, 4 – agree, 5 – strongly agree).

The results (Table 7) show that respondents, when engaged in adventure activities, immensely value the following motives: escapism from everyday life, boredom avoidance, the thrill of an adventure, the experience of new things, adrenalin, pleasure and joy, fun, happiness, challenge, social contacts, natural resources and contact with nature, attractiveness of destination and different cultures. They are also, to a lesser extent, driven by the motives of: novelty in life, competence, self-discovery, passion for adventures, empowerment, self-reward, freedom, spirit regeneration and authenticity. The least associated reasons with adventure activities' engagement are danger, risk and status achievement. Concerning the gender differences, it seems that women, unlike men, also value the motives of sensation-seeking, self-fulfilment, personal growth, self-discovery, self-actualisation, empowerment and freedom; some think they are born for adventures, have passion for adventures and adventures represent who they are.

Q5) What kind of a person are you? How would you describe yourself?

Respondents described themselves as curious, open, fearless, resourceful, empathetic, persistent, liking challenges and moving personal limits, sincere, cheerful, adventurous, knowledge-seeking, straightforward, friendly and ready to help.

Q6) Do you engage in adventure activities alone or with other people?

Respondents mainly engage in adventure activities with others for community and sharing feelings, whereas some adventure activities are done individually (e.g. cycling, paddle surfing and some travels).

Q7) Do you usually stick with your familiar adventure activities, or are you prone to try out some new/other adventure activities?

Respondents usually stick with familiar/favourite adventure activities. However, they are prone to occasionally try other novel adventure activities if they do not involve a high risk or life/health endangerment. One respondent always prefers new adventures.

Q8) What do you think about the following adventure activities: (1) lighthouse stay, (2) solo travel, (3) dark tourism (travel to places historically associated with death and tragedy)? How attractive are they to you; which ones would you try; what do you expect from them?

Respondents found lighthouse stays attractive and dark tourism challenging, however, not as a solo trip. One respondent prefers all three adventures (lighthouse stay, solo travel and dark tourism).

From these activities, they would expect unique experiences, quietness and calmness, a special atmosphere, escapism from everyday life, excitement (e.g. from lighthouse stay), personal growth, confidence and complete freedom (e.g. from solo travels), deeper connections and better history, culture and people understanding, exciting stories (e.g. from dark tourism). All three mentioned activities are perceived as offering opportunities for exploration, self-knowledge and memory creation. One respondent is not fond of solo travels and dark tourism due to perceiving them as sad. Another respondent was engaged in dark tourism and perceives such activities as disturbing.

To sum up, concerning gender, adventure- and risk-prone individuals share many motives for engaging in adventure activities, but slight differences exist. Namely, women tend to have motives that are different from men's. Sharing reasons involve escapism from everyday life, boredom avoidance, the thrill of an adventure, the experience of new things, adrenalin, pleasure and joy, fun, happiness, challenge, social contacts, natural resources and contact with nature, attractiveness of destination and different cultures. The least attractive reasons for adventure activities include danger, risk and status achievement. Some of these motives align with the existing theoretical insights elaborated earlier, while some (e.g. the least attractive) provide novel findings.

Chapter 6

Development of a Specialised Tourism Product and Market Testing

6.1. Prototype and Prototype Development

At this stage of the development of a new specialised tourism product, the future tourism content is fully formed. It is no longer a newly developed idea, a virtual representation, descriptive features and the like. The findings from all the previously conducted analyses are combined into a final content that meets the required quality standards. In this phase, the final conception of the new content is transformed into a tourism product with a specific price and characteristics. The first step in this phase is the design of the prototype of the new tourist service. This presupposes the offer of content in a real environment where it is continuously offered to tourists. The reactions of tourists during the provision of a new service are analysed. Tourists are observed in the real environment to evaluate their experience and satisfaction with the new content. For simple specialised tourism products, one prototype is sufficient. Based on the experience and comments of tourists trying out the product, the final form of the new specialised tourism product is determined. For more complex specialised tourism products, several prototypes can be developed. Prototypes differ in the degree of logistical support in providing a new service. The prototype of a new specialised tourism product is always analysed in the environment where the service will be provided.

Regardless of the level of completeness of the prototype, the content offered should provide a complete experience of the new service. The development of prototypes of a new tangible product at a lower level is carried out in the virtual sphere, as a computer simulation, due to lower costs. The prototype of a specific tourism product should be developed in a real, physical form. The problem of relative intangibility of the tourism service is solved by providing a service, so it is advisable to do the same in the development of prototypes (Borja de Mozota, 2003; Buhalis & Foerste, 2015; Neumeier, 2009; Šerić, Ljubica, et al., 2015).

The prototype of a new specialised tourism product is considered by the authors in their own practice before it is offered to tourists with selected tourism representatives (from agencies expected to sell the product) and tourism journalists.

Specialised Tourism Products, 79–87
Copyright © 2024 Neven Šerić, Ivana Kursan Milaković and Ivan Peronja
Published under exclusive licence by Emerald Publishing Limited
doi:10.1108/978-1-83549-408-020241006

Case study 5 argues the usefulness of prototyping for new specialised tourism products. Regardless of the considerations of the creators of the new tourism product, the reactions of the interested tourist population will vary according to secondary (e.g. the characteristics of the environment of the place of stay) and tertiary characteristics (e.g. the duration of the transfer, the availability of the place of stay, etc.). Because this was prototype testing, the apartments in which participants in the experiment stayed were neither fully equipped nor categorised. The participants who did not care which lighthouse they stayed in (alpha prototype) cared about the primary promotional features (seclusion in century-old buildings surrounded by a preserved landscape). The beta prototype was used in the experiment to learn about the impressions and experiences of a tourist stay in lighthouses close to civilisation and the gamma prototype for the same purpose by staying at isolated, hard-to-reach offshore destinations. In the prototyping of specialised tourism products, the level of completion/completeness of the content is determined according to the expectations of the tourist segment that has opted for a particular variant.

Case Study 5: Elaboration of Prototypes for the Tourist Service, Stay in the Lighthouse

During the development of a special tourism product – a stay in a lighthouse – the initial prototype was created on the basis of an experiment in which students and teachers from the Polytechnic in Split stayed at two different lighthouses in several groups for 7 days. During the previous stages of the development of this specialised tourism product, the basic features defined a stay in an isolated location, accommodation in a building of cultural and historical heritage in the environment of a preserved landscape. During the experiment with students and teachers of Polytechnic in Split, three prototypes of this new tourist offer were used.

The alpha prototype contained written information with a video presentation and photos of two lighthouses in different environments (one on an offshore island, the other on a larger inhabited island with accessible civilisation and supplies). The offer was presented to the students in person by the project manager, who shared his own experiences during his stay at the lighthouses. The workshop was held with the students in the order in which they chose one or the other lighthouse offered. For the beta prototype, the Stončica lighthouse on the island of Vis (Fig. 4) was chosen, which is connected by a road to the small town of Vis, where it is possible to get a full supply of food and other necessities, and given the daily boat connection between Vis and Split, any participant in the experiment could end their stay and leave the lighthouse at any time.

For the gamma prototype, a lighthouse was chosen on the offshore island of Sučac (Fig. 5), where there is no possibility of supplies and departure is possible only after a 7-day stay, when return transfer was organised.

The prototypes were presented in three separate workshops attended by the same group of students. The questions, dilemmas and comments of the students and their teachers were recorded and analysed, and this written material was used in the analysis of the participants of the experiment who chose the beta/ gamma prototype, i.e. those who in principle declared that they were interested in staying in the lighthouse (alpha prototype), but the final decision would be made after the information of those who would go to Stončica on Vis, i.e. to Sušac in the first group, was passed on to them.

Based on the communication of each of the presented prototypes, the determination of the workshop participants for each of them and the impressions they expressed after a 7-day stay in the selected lighthouse, various concepts for the promotion of the stay in the lighthouse were formed, which were later used in the presentation of all lighthouses renovated for tourist stays. Based on the experience of the experiment, the structure and quantity of recommended food for a 7-day stay per person were determined, the recommended days of the week for transfers were determined, the average consumption of sanitary and drinking water per person was determined and consequently the required capacity of absorption/biological pits where sanitary wastewater is disposed of. Methods for classification, recycling of recyclable waste and transportation of non-recyclable waste were determined. Rules were established for the conduct of guests while in the lighthouse, as it is a safety facility for navigation. Guidelines were also established for lighthouse keepers regarding their relationship and communication with guests during their stay at the lighthouse.

The development and testing of three different prototypes of a new specialised tourism product eliminated many dilemmas. According to the experience gained from the experiment with the students and teachers of the Polytechnic in Split, even today, 20 years after the marketing of this new tourist offer, there are no complaints or comments from guests in the impression books.

The alpha prototype of a specialised tourism product can be used as an outline of the basic features sufficient for original promotion and presentation of the basic added value (in the specific case, a tourist stay in an isolated destination, accommodation in a historic building, a preserved landscape). In this sense, the alpha prototype in advertising does not imply a detailed elaboration of the secondary and especially not of the tertiary characteristics of the specialised tourism product. For this reason, it is risky to rely exclusively on the alpha prototype in the other stages of the development of a new specialised tourism product, as this may also lead to misunderstanding the real attractiveness of the content offered. The alpha prototype of a new specialised tourism product can be used for the development of other prototypes that are able to provide more relevant insights into the impressions of potential tourists and determine the main characteristics of certain subcategories of specialised tourism products that should be prioritised for promotion. The alpha prototype of the new specialised

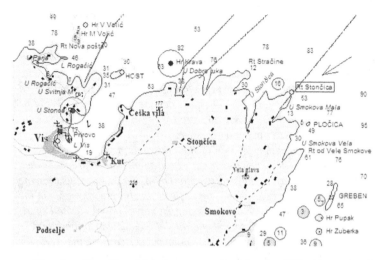

Fig. 4.   Stončica Lighthouse on the Island of Vis (Arrow). *Source:*
Author's archive.

tourism product should allow the actual interaction of the people involved in the experiment with the core content. The alpha prototype should be used to clarify doubts and dilemmas related to the totality of the tourism content and the necessary logistical support in the provision of an integrated tourism service (from arrival, during stay and return). Beta and gamma prototypes of a new specialised tourism product should provide a more complete insight into all features of the specific content.

The impressions of the alpha prototype from people exposed to the experiment will be more intense if the specialised tourism product is already branded, as was the case with this new tourist content that the media has already informed the public about. This experience has shown that the awareness of a new specialised tourist offer contributes to the growth of demand.

6.2. Testing the Prototype

To test the prototype of a new specialised tourism product, it is advisable to select people who are informed about the new content that will be offered. Since tourism is a specific social phenomenon, it is not advisable to leave the testing of prototypes of new content to marketing agencies that usually deal with market testing activities. Prototype testing is a phase that is carried out when it is decided that a new tourist content should be presented to the public. In this way, a lot of useful information can be obtained about the perception and experience of new content in the consciousness and subconsciousness of tourists.

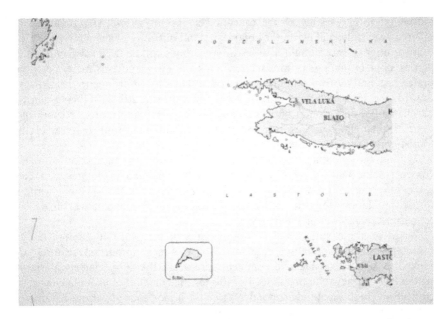

Fig. 5.   The Sušac Lighthouse on the Island of the Same Name (in the
Square). *Source:* Author's archive.

The first prototype of a new content to be tested should always be an alpha concept. Regardless of the level of completeness of the new tourism content and the type of prototype testing (in a selected location or virtually), the use of an alpha prototype reduces the cost of higher prototype levels (beta, gamma) and the overall process of developing a new offering. The findings on respondents' impressions of the alpha prototype of the new tourist offer determine its characteristics that are most important for tourists in terms of experience (contributing to positive emotions, creation of loyalty to the new specialised tourist offer, etc.).

Thanks to the development of virtual possibilities and neuromarketing tools, testing the alpha prototype of a new tourism product does not have to be carried out in the actual physical place where it will be offered. It is important to provide respondents with the basic features of the new tourism product and analyse their impressions of its characteristics and attractiveness.

Testing of the beta prototype of the new specialised tourism product is conducted in the place where it will actually be offered. The location contributes to the overall impression of the new offering, so the results of this test provide a more comprehensive view of the respondents' experience. The experience of each tourist content in the real environment is more intense, and the comments of the participants in this experiment are more complete. In this way, more useful recommendations will be known in relation to the individual characteristics of the new tourist offer. The testing of the tourism beta prototype will be conducted in different ways, depending on the complexity and difficulty of the new specialised tourism offer. Various qualitative research methods will be used (respondents' e-diaries, content analysis of tourists' reactions, etc.) to identify as many potential preferences and motives of tourists as possible that may contribute to their loyalty towards the new specialised tourist offer (Šerić & Jurišić, 2014). In their e-diaries, which can be kept on smartphones as part of the offered application, respondents describe their daily impressions and impressions about certain features of the tourist content offered to them.

Testing the gamma prototype implies an even more specific or complete content of the new specialised tourist offer. The gamma prototype of a new specialised tourism product represents the completeness of the offer but without formal regulations (e.g. no tourist categorisation of the content was made, no tourist insurances were regulated, etc.).

Based on the experience of the participants of the beta and gamma test of prototypes of the specialised tourism offer, the most important features are ranked, and possible negative comments are argued with special emphasis on particularly attractive impressions. For this test, the method of *indivisible marks* is convenient. In this method, respondents rate the importance of various features of the new tourist offer on a scale (1–10). The ratings indicate the degree of attractiveness of a particular feature.

6.3. Testing the Tourist Market

Testing the tourist market represents a kind of further development of the prototype testing of a new specialised tourism product. The fundamental difference lies in the selection of respondents. For prototype testing, respondents who are familiar with the specifics of the new tourism product are selected, while for tourism market testing, random tourists are selected. If the knowledge of the reactions and impressions of the respondents exposed to the prototype testing experiment is sufficient to resolve the remaining dilemmas and doubts regarding the final, complete content of the offer, it is not necessary to conduct the tourist market testing. However, if there are still certain dilemmas regarding some features of the future tourist offer, it is advisable to conduct a test on the tourist market. Testing on the tourist market will also reveal the functional characteristics of the new content that are particularly attractive to different tourist segments. The assumption is that by testing the prototype, it has been determined that there are no more *irreparable flaws* in the content of the presented concept – features that would deter potential tourists in some way (for example, when offering a tourist stay in the lighthouse, that the fear of the target tourist group of staying on isolated offshore islands has been completely eliminated).

In the testing phase of a new specialised tourism product, first the method and the number of tourists are determined, then the duration of this activity and the institution conducting it. Conducting tests of the tourist market in connection with new specialised tourist content is carried out virtually or in reality in modern practice. Virtual testing of the tourist market involves a computer simulation in which new tourist content is presented and offered to selected respondents in the form of a contest along with selected contest content. Respondents are asked to choose one of the offers and explain the reasons for their decision. In practice, this type of tourism market testing can be done through the intermediation of travel agencies with which cooperation already exists, but more often it is done in-house. One or more target markets for target tourism are selected. Often these are those that are expected to make up the bulk of the future clientele that will choose specific tourism content. This concept of testing the tourism market can be classified as pseudo-sales (Hedin et al., 2011). The use of *pseudo-sales* allows for a short period of time, and the necessary data can be collected during the month of implementation. The authors use the *controlled sales* model in their own practice (Šerić & Marušić, 2019). *Controlled sales* are often conducted over 3 months. This model implies real reservations of a new specialised tourist service on the offered terms, but in a limited volume. Market tests are conducted based on reservations, but they do not require advance payment. The obligation to pay for the reservation arises only when the interested tourist who made the reservation a few days before the offered date contacts the provider of the new tourist service and makes the payment for it. During the provision of a new specialised tourist service, tourists' impressions and their subsequent comments are recorded.

Recently, testing the tourist market through *complete sales* is becoming more common. In this model, there are no limits; the reservation implies the payment of an advance or even the entire amount by a certain date. The duration of the implementation of such a market test depends on the time (days (months)) in which the reservation can be cancelled, and the amount paid can be refunded. In practice, it is carried out similarly to the model of controlled sale. The model of the *complete sale* in market tests is identical to the formal sale of any tourist service.

Based on the reactions, reservations, questions, and dilemmas of the respondents, recommended changes in content, ways of providing new offer and other information useful for the final marketing are identified, regardless of the model of market testing implementation. Tourism market testing requires promotional activities tailored to the selected model to entice the target tourism clientele to participate.

Tactics for market testing in tourism are:

- *sales wave observation;*
- *simulated trial marketing;*
- *controlled marketing test of the attractiveness of the offer;*
- *analysis of test markets.*

Sales wave tracking involves a test offer of a new specialised tourist service offered at a discount to interested tourists. The discount decreases with the weeks the offer is open. It is highest in the first week after the offer is announced. The specific tourist offer is advertised in *waves*, not continuously during the market test, although it is possible to make a reservation during this entire period. By *observing the sales wave*, the attractiveness of the new tourist offer and the required intensity of advertising are determined. In the weeks when promotional activities are carried out, it is possible to analyse the sales waves with selected metrics and thus know the specific contribution of different promotional activities to the achieved sales (Šerić & Luetić, 2016). This tactic is used to test the market by *controlled* or *direct* selling. The implementation is simple, and the knowledge about the impressions of the tourist demand in relation to the new specialised tourism product is relevant for the remaining stages and commercialisation, i.e. the introduction of a new service on the market.

The *simulated test marketing* is carried out on a sample of 30–40 interested tourists. The sample is selected in cooperation with sales agents in strategic outbound markets. The sales agent informs the tourists included in the sample about the content of the new specialised tourist offer. Then a survey is conducted among the respondents. Their opinions and attitudes about the offered content and its price are questioned. Based on the answers, the intensity of interest in making a reservation or a test purchase is determined. The data collected through the questionnaire provide information about the personal preferences of the respondents towards the offered category of a specialised tourism product. The tactic is used to test the market according to the models of *pseudo, controlled* and *complete sales*. In *pseudo-sales*, more variations are possible. For example, respondents may be given a notional amount of money to spend according to their personal preferences on the various specialty tourism products offered, which include the offer for which the market test is being conducted. The alternatives offered do not have to be from the same category of specialised tourism products. The intensity of the respondents' commitment to the offer for which the test is conducted is analysed. Based on the results, it is possible to realistically estimate the required intensity of promotional activities before and during the marketing of the new specialised tourist offer.

A *controlled marketing test* is carried out through several sales agents in several radiating tourism markets at the same time. Nothing is proposed to the sales agents, but they are free to present new tourist content to their loyal tourist clientele. Respondents' reactions to the content offered are analysed, as well as the effectiveness of different approaches to presenting and promoting it by different sales agents. In particular, the impressions about the price of the offered contents are investigated. Through a *controlled marketing test*, it is possible to determine the contribution of different methods of promotion and sales to the creation of a positive attitude of the target tourist population towards the offered content. However, this tactic comprehensively exposes the new tourist offer to the findings of all types of competition.

Test market analysis is conducted through identical advertising of new tourism content on several selected tourism target markets simultaneously. Advertising is conducted by sales representatives in these markets, but strictly according to the guidelines of the tourism company developing the new content.

Testing of tourist markets can be done exclusively with a selected sales representative (following Kerin & Peterson, 2004). In this scenario, *alpha* and *beta* prototypes of a new specialised tourism product and the full concept of the same are presented to its sales representatives. Respondents freely express their impressions and suggestions regarding the presented prototype.

When conducting market tests in tourism, it is important to keep in mind that respondents' reactions are influenced by the perception of the tourism company offering new content, i.e. the awareness of its brand in the global tourism market (Šerić, Jakšić Stojanović, et al., 2023). Market testing is more efficient when the new tourism content is already known as a brand. This was also confirmed by the author's experience with the *Stone Lights* project. When developing this brand, the authors tried to combine the characteristics of the conspiracy theory, the predominant blue colour (sea), the stone (historical buildings – stone towers with lights) and the original innovative tourist offer (*new light in Croatian tourism*) – pictorial characteristics of the *Stone Lights* brand. In the author's practice, the selected pictorial characteristics of this brand have proven to be an additional motivating factor, both in market tests and in the commercialisation of the offer. From these experiences, it can be concluded that the image features of the brand adapted to the marketing story contribute to the credibility of the presented content of the new specialised tourism product.

It is advisable to present the new specialised tourism product in an authentic way, with as many characteristics and attractive elements as possible. The scope of testing the tourist market is determined in accordance with the budget allocated for that purpose. The implementation period will be determined according to the way the tests are carried out, taking care to create a relevant sample (typical representatives of the target tourist population). Insights into tourists' impressions during the market test and, in particular, the number of actual bookings when using the model and tactics that predict the same contribute to a detailed insight into the attractiveness and competitiveness of the new tourist content and the intensity of the promotion of *test purchases*. By testing the tourist market, valuable information is obtained about the perception of the new tourist offer by the tourist target segments and the sales intermediaries whose employees are involved in this process.

Chapter 7

Tourism Product Policy and Sales Policy

7.1. Policy of the Specialised Tourism Product

The policy of a specialised tourism product would be based on the need for which the new content is primarily intended. The sales policy of a new offer should be based on its vision and mission and take into account the product policy. During development, the policy of a new tourism product is modified by the marketing strategy chosen and later, after commercialisation, by life cycle management activities (Kotler et al., 2009). The policy of the tourism product is based on the resources of the company that develops and markets it. It adapts to the standards of the category of specialised tourism products to which it belongs. With the product policy, the tourism company establishes the organisation of provision, coordination and control of all activities during the development and later after the launch. The policy of a specialised tourism product that meets the market environment and the needs of the target tourism segments contributes to the competitive positioning, the dynamics of tourism acceptance and loyalty and the dissemination of information about the tourism offer in the global market.

Prerequisites for an effective tourism product policy are an effective marketing information system and an effective organisational structure for the provision of tourism services, as well as effective internal and external communication. Product policy has a significant impact on the attractiveness and sales.

Tourism product policy should be the basis for all management activities. Its importance is particularly expressed in the phase of introduction and marketing of a new specialised tourism product (Šerić & Jurišić, 2014). It is advisable to treat the launch and marketing of a new tourism product differently in terms of promotion (Šerić, 2016). The launch of a new tourism product represents its physical positioning on the market. Commercialisation begins with its sale. How tourists and competitors will ultimately react to the new specialised tourism product depends on the adaptation of the product policy to the existing supply and demand conditions. The policy of the specialised tourism product is a recommended starting point for the sales policy and sales strategy. The dynamics of acceptance and the life cycle of a new specialised tourism product depend on all these factors.

Specialised Tourism Products, 89–94
Copyright © 2024 Neven Šerić, Ivana Kursan Milaković and Ivan Peronja
Published under exclusive licence by Emerald Publishing Limited
doi:10.1108/978-1-83549-408-020241007

7.2. Sales Policies

After the knowledge gained through market testing, especially in relation to price dilemmas, the selection of the sales policy for a new specialised tourism product is tackled. The first option is the selection of the sales policy practised by the tourist unit for the existing contents of its offer. This choice helps to strengthen the image of the tourist entity, since the new offer is perceived as an added value. An alternative is the commitment to a specific sales policy based on the findings about the impressions of the new contents (results of the market tests). This commitment can further strengthen the image of originality of the new specialised tourism product. The sales policy has a significant impact on test purchase, acceptance and loyalty towards to a new tourism product (adapted from Czinkota, 2000; Grbac et al., 2008; Hooley et al., 2004; Laws, 2002; Šerić & Luetić, 2016).

Sales policies are concretised principles for selling tourism products. Sales policies are all sales tactics, sales programmes and sales measures that are undertaken to successfully introduce, market and maintain demand throughout the life cycle of a specific tourism product. It is recommended to adapt the sales policy to the basic characteristics of the new specialised tourism product and to the target segment of tourists. Sales policy has an effect on the lifespan of any product, including tourism products (Šerić, 2009b). The right choice of sales policy will contribute to the growth of sales and market share of the new tourist service. In order for the selection of sales policies to be relevant to the market environment, up-to-date information on competing tourism products, tourists' attitudes towards them, data on the structure of tourists in the receptive market, standards and opinions of sales agents on existing B2B practices and other knowledge are needed.

The effectiveness of the sales policy depends on the activities that precede the sale, as well as everything that happens after the sales activity. A well-chosen sales policy also helps to strengthen the image of the tourist facility among tourists, sales intermediaries and all stakeholders in the supply chain. The tourist facility selects the sales policies in accordance with:

- the depth and breadth of the range of its products and services;
- marketing activities to support the sale;
- the service provided before and after the sale;
- the existing sales system;
- the pricing policy practised.

It is also justified to choose sales policies that contribute to the optimisation of the sales function and the sales activities of the tourism company. However, it is important that they are consistent with the business standards of the target markets. For this reason, it is not advisable to have an identical sales policy in all target markets. This rule should be observed especially in outbound markets where business is conducted exclusively through local sales representatives (agencies). The choice of sales policy should be left to them.

Depending on the period of implementation, sales policies are classified as short term, medium term and long term. Both the policy for the new tourism product and the sales policy should be aligned with the marketing strategy of the tourism facility.

They are organisationally aligned with the tourism entity's business, financial and legal policies. They should also be coordinated with the policy of the tourist entity's offer and the brand of the new specialised tourism product. In modern tourism practice, the following strategies for selling specialised tourism products are recognised:

- Sales policies based on extreme features of the specialised tourist content. They additionally promote the originality and exclusivity of the specific offer and are an argument for a premium addition to the price. Customers are ultimately satisfied with the possibility of buying a tourism product and are not too price sensitive.
- Sales policy based on the policy of promoting rare, valuable resources on which the specialised tourist service or offer is based. If the resources are truly rare and preserved, this adds to the exclusivity of the offer and can be included in the markup on the price of a new specialised tourism product.
- The sales policy based on the branding of a specialty tourism product respects the existing market perception and brand awareness of the company that will sell it (Keller, 2003). For this reason, associations with higher prices (sales agents are specialised travel agencies) and lower prices (sales agents are large tour operators) are possible.
- Sales policy based on the brand policy of the tourism company that will sell the new specialised tourism product. The existing market image of the tourism company is transferred to the image of the new specialised tourism product. This can have both a positive and negative impact on the impression of the price of the content offered.
- Sales policy based on the brand policy, which is aligned with the strategic business objectives of the tourism company. They are defined according to the depth and breadth of the existing offer and the target niche in which the new specialised tourism product will be offered. The aim is to achieve greater differentiation of the new specialised tourism product, which implies the adoption of a higher price premium.
- Sales policy based on the pricing policy of the tourism company in accordance with its market image and the perception of the existing offer by tourists.
- Sales policy based on the discount policy respects the standards of discounts granted to sales intermediaries with whom we already cooperate.
- The sales policy based on the existing sales channels and business standards with sales intermediaries.

The selection of a new sales policy for specialised tourism products also depends on the existing market relations between supply and demand, the purchasing power of the target tourist clientele and other relevant variables in the tourism business (Buhalis, 2022; Šerić, 2003; Šerić & Luković, 2007). It is useful to analyse the content and prices of competing and substituting specialised tourism products, as well as the sales policies practised by competitors (Meler, 2010). Based on all these findings, sales policies are selected that can ensure the growth and maintenance of market share as long as possible during the lifespan of the specialised tourism product. In their own business practice, the authors apply the following sales strategies for specialised tourism products:

- Cooperation policy of stakeholders in the sale and provision of specialised tourist services – defines relationships and forms of cooperation. This policy helps to reduce the cost of developing, marketing, positioning and providing specialised tourism services.
- The policy for monitoring the sale of a new specialised tourism product (detailed records for selecting tactical decisions in sales management).
- The strategic policy for the growth of sales of a new specialised tourism product defines tactics that can additionally stimulate demand (discounts for multiple purchases, reduced price per person for groups, etc.). This policy can target additional tourist segments, analyse the sustainability of sales in the chosen niche and explore alternative market niches, improve the existing ones and introduce new promotional activities, connect with new sales intermediaries, etc...
- The trade fair policy establishes the criteria for selecting the tourist trade fairs where the specialised tourism product will be presented and the way in which this will be implemented.
- Trade secrecy policy related to the development and marketing of a new specialised tourism product specifies what should not be disclosed to the public until the launch of a new tourism service. This policy defines the methods and responsibilities for documenting the development of a new specialised tourism product.
- The policy for selecting sales personnel defines the criteria that must be met by personnel involved in the sale of specialised tourism products.
- The policy for the selection of personnel involved in the provision of specialised tourist services. Within this policy, the additional training of the same personnel during the life cycle of a new tourism product is established.
- The policy of competition in the sale of a new specialised tourism product establishes additional incentives for the sales agents depending on the realisation of the sales plan.
- The policy of approval of changes in a new specialised tourism product defines who, when and to what extent can make decisions on content deviations and the way of providing a new tourist service during its lifetime.
- The franchise policy defines the price and conditions for transferring the right to offer a legally protected specialised tourism product.
- The policy of auditing marketing activities defines the activities that will be monitored and, if necessary, proposes changes to increase their sales efficiency.

- The policy of coordinating contacts with tourists and tourist intermediaries sets the standards for communication with the tourist public, especially with sales intermediaries, to further boost sales.
- The policy of interviewing tourists who decide to use a new specialised tourism product establishes the time periods and the manner in which these interviews will be conducted.
- The policy of taking care of the users of the new tourism product before and after the sale combines the recommended activities to prepare tourists to be even more satisfied.
- The policy of communication with competitors establishes the way of cooperation with local competitors offering contents of the same category of specialised tourism products, with the aim of strengthening the image and synergy of the specialised tourist offer of the destination and extending the tourist season.
- The policy for the promotion of a new specialised tourism product has the task of binding tourists to the offer and strengthening the image of the same and of the company that offers it.
- The policy of tourist safety defines the potential threats to tourists during the provision of specialised tourist services and protective measures, as well as the necessary insurance policies.
- The policy of discounts and rebates defines the possibilities of additional incentives for sales agents on the price of a new specialised tourism product.
- The advertising policy defines the budget and media activities to promote the sale of a new specialised tourism product in the introduction and marketing phase and during its life cycle.

When choosing a sales policy for a new specialised tourism product, efforts should be made to maintain a balance of sales dynamics during the planned life cycle of the specific content in accordance with the sales plan. The presented sales policies, practised and proposed by the authors in their own projects, are the starting points for the development of modified and completely new sales policies, adapted to specific specialised tourism products. Continuous improvement of existing and development of new sales policies is a prerequisite for extending the life of a specialised tourist offer. Sales strategies for specialised tourism products should be adapted to the targeted strategic tourism markets and promoted with appropriate advertising. The *Stone Lights* project went a step further and promoted different sales policies for narrower segments of a broadcast market. For example, advertising for the target segment of ADAC Germany members was developed through the *Reisemagazin*. For the customers of the German travel agency ID RIVA TOURS, which specialises in offers in the Republic of Croatia, the sales policy is promoted through the annual catalogue.

For the policy of selling specialised tourism products to be effective and efficient, a synergy of all elements of the marketing mix is required. The pricing strategy should be in accordance with the experience of the specific offer; the sale should be organised through intermediaries and partners competent not only for that category of content but also for the target segments of tourists. Finally, the advertising mix should be aligned with the other components of the marketing mix, even differentiated for different segments of the same tourist market.

Chapter 8

Introduction of a Specialised Tourism Product on the Market

The market launch of a new specialised tourism product practically takes place in two phases, the market launch (and positioning) and the commercialisation. The market launch of the new tourist offer has formally begun when the prototype testing has not taken place without the insight of the general public. Regardless of the alternative chosen, the public will become familiar with the new content to be offered to tourists during the market test. Therefore, targeted advertising to strategically important tourist markets, strategic segments of tourists taking into account their preferences, etc. is recommended (Moss & Atre, 2003).

The launch phase implies the introduction of new tourist content as a concrete offer, where the characteristics and price are completely clear and an added value is recommended (in the case of a tourist stay in the lighthouse – the uniqueness of the ambience of remote offshore oases, the exceptional cleanliness of the sea, the opportunity to enjoy special gastronomic delicacies, some of which I cannot find even in the best restaurants, etc.). In accordance with the specifics of the primary (stay in the lighthouse, accommodation in historic buildings), secondary (possibility to enjoy autochthonous eco-gastronomic specialties) and tertiary characteristics of the specialised offer, a market niche is selected in which it will position itself permanently.

Commercialisation implies the continuous diffusion of new tourist offers in the global tourism market. Dissemination is the process of distributing complete information about a new specialised tourist offer and its distribution through selected intermediaries and their distribution channels.

The introduction and marketing of a new specialised tourism product is carried out independently by the tourist entity if it has the appropriate experience and resources. In practice, the tourist entity often works with partners responsible for selling and promoting specific categories of tourist content and specific markets of outbound tourism. In certain scenarios, the launch and marketing may be left entirely to selected sales intermediaries, either in receptive or targeted outbound tourism markets. All activities carried out during the launch and marketing phase of a new specialised tourism product should promote and contribute to the

Specialised Tourism Products, 95–101
Copyright © 2024 Neven Šerić, Ivana Kursan Milaković and Ivan Peronja
Published under exclusive licence by Emerald Publishing Limited
doi:10.1108/978-1-83549-408-020241008

acceptance of the new specialised tourism product. At the same time, selected promotional activities are carried out in accordance with the previously established marketing strategy, plan and programme. At this stage, promotional activities should be chosen that primarily contribute to raising the profile of the new tourism product. In addition, preference should be given to activities that encourage tourists to test new content.

Tourists evaluate new content based on the information available to them about the offer, features and price. This information should be clearly communicated through selected promotional activities (Best, 2010; Keller, 2003).

The acceptance of new content, products or services and the creation of loyalty towards them is not instantaneous (Cavalcanti, 2005; Jakšić Stojanović et al., 2019a; Piercy, 2002; Rocco & Pisnik, 2014). There are many reasons for this, and some are related to clients' ethical standards (Andreasen, 2001; Meler & Ham, 2012; Mihić & Šerić, 2007). In the author's practice, it has been shown that it takes longer to accept new tourist content that is more complex in terms of content and performance (experience with tourist accommodation in lighthouses, with tourist accommodation in monasteries, etc.). This is also indicated by recent theories that follow the research of others (Buhalis & Park, 2021; Buhalis & Sinarta, 2019; Nunkoo et al., 2019 and others). Some features of a new specialised tourism product may help to more quickly arouse the interest of the tourist segment that socialises with them, but the first purchase will occur only after the tourist has overcome their dilemmas and possible fears (promised quality, etc.).

In contrast to more complex new tourism content, evaluating a new offer that is simple in terms of content and performance will take less time.

The repeated purchase of complex and simple new tourist content depends on adapting to the habits, behaviours and trends of the target segments of tourists. Due to the aforementioned facts, it is not advisable to target a wider population with a new specialised tourism product. Compromises in adapting content and performance to a larger number of tourist segments lead to an increase in the time span for first-time and repeat purchases. This has been confirmed by the authors' practice (Šerić, 2019b; Šerić & Jurišić, 2015; Šerić & Marušić, 2019; Šerić, Mihanović, et al., 2020; Šerić, Peronja, et al., 2020). The dynamics of creating loyalty for a simple and for a complex, specialised tourism product will largely depend on the impressions after the first, *trial purchase*. For this reason, it is important that sales personnel assigned to the launch phase of a new specialised tourism product have the expertise and experience to adequately promote the features of the offer and ensure high-quality performance. In the case of certain content (tourist content based on extreme sports and special skills of tourists), it is important that its providers contribute to the tourists' sense of safety (in the *Stone Lights* project, special attention was paid to the crews of fast boats engaged for tourist transfers to offshore islands). Commercialisation of a new specialised tourism product requires the introduction of new content into the wider sales system of the global tourism market. This process should be supported by marketing activities adapted to the specifics of the new tourism content. Digital marketing is suitable for this purpose, as it allows detailed information about the target tourist group. Marketing support will also contribute to increase the interest of potential intermediaries (Bilandžić, 2008; Borges et al., 2009; Ramsdell, 2002). A tourist facility that launches a new product chooses a niche where the specific content has good visibility. Today, the visibility of new tourist content is additionally encouraged by the implementation of sustainable tourism standards (controlled intensity of tourist visits, etc.). The visibility of the new tourism content in the selected niche is also promoted by the fact that the characteristics of the offer are in line with the standards of other offers within the same market niche (e.g. ecological standards – preservation of landscapes, native species, cultural and historical heritage, etc.).

There are additional costs associated with marketing a new specialised tourism product. Additional targeted promotional efforts are required (targeting a specific strategic segment of tourists who are believed to be the first to make a test purchase).

When marketing a new specialised tourism product, it is important to highlight its unique characteristics. Especially those that contribute significantly to making it stand out from the existing tourist offer. The messages should be clear and include information on where and through which sales agents the offered content can be reserved. Everything that was defined in the phase of designing and creating the marketing strategy is now communicated to the target tourist audience. The marketing strategy is tailored to the specifics of the target tourist population. However, as the conditions in the tourism market and the preferences of tourists change, it may be necessary to modify the way of implementing the marketing strategy at this final stage. Promotional activities should be developed in accordance with the ethical standards that apply to the targeted emitting tourist markets (tourists who are believed to make up the majority of those who quickly decide to make a test purchase). It is useful to remember the existing standards and norms that contribute to the creation of loyalty among the target clientele (Andreasen, 2001; Barros & Mascarenhas, 2005; Churchill, 2002; Mihić & Šerić, 2007). The adaptation of promotional activities to the new specialised tourist offer contributes to the increase of interest of the tourist public and to the increase of sales, i.e. to the transition from the phase of market introduction to the phase of market growth. During this transition, it is advisable to analyse and further adapt the existing logistical support for the sale and provision of new services to achieve the established sales plan, now in a real market environment.

In their own practice, the authors opt for one of the models of commercialisation of new specialised tourism products:

(1) model of early entry;
(2) model of parallel entry;
(3) model of later market entry.

- Ad1) The early entry model is practiced when the new specialised tourism offer has been worked out in detail in terms of content and marketing in the previous development stages. Through the continuous exchange of ideas and information with sales intermediaries, most of the dilemmas could be solved. Early market entry with a new tourism product enables advantages over new offerings from competitors in the target market (especially in the destination where the new content is offered). The decision to enter the market early also reduces the risk that one of the local competitors will copy all or part of the new tourism offering. Another argument for early entry is the need to regulate special permits (e.g. concessions for maritime property or some other resources). An argument for choosing the early market entry model is the complexity of providing and logistical support for the new tourist offer (e.g. special organisation of transfer for hard-to-reach places). The early market entry model is also recommended for all specialised tourism products based on valuable landscape and other destination resources, which represent an innovation in the destination's offer, etc. If the marketing of a new specialised tourist offer requires a special additional infrastructure, the visibility for competitors is obvious, so it is recommended to monitor whether any of them develops a similar variant of such tourist offer. In such a market scenario, the dilemma of whether to further accelerate commercialisation should be resolved. Faster implementation of commercialisation than planned may result in lower quality of the new tourism service. The right decision is made based on the assessment of the similarity of the main features of the new tourist service with the competitor's service. Faster implementation of marketing than planned may also lead to errors in communication with the target tourist group. This risk is high if there is no relevant information about the perception of the vision of the new specialised tourism product (market test). Insufficient knowledge about the possible impressions of the shortcomings of the new tourist offer in the early entry scenario can also be caused by negative publicity. Its reach through the social networks can lead to a complete business collapse of the new tourist offer. In this way, competitors have the opportunity to present and position themselves appropriately on the tourism market based on the bad experiences of others, even if the offer is later marketed with similar characteristics. Taking into account all the presented facts, the model of early entry into the tourism market with a new offer is associated with a high business risk.

- Ad2) The model of parallel entry, i.e. launching a new specialised tourism product in parallel with the marketing of new tourism content by other stakeholders, including new receptive units in the destination (new hotels, camps, etc.), is recommended for offers with original features. Through other new contents and offers in the same destination, a synergy is created that attracts the attention of the tourist public. If the development of new outbound markets takes place at the same time, the parallel introduction of a new specialised tourism product also allows experimentation with completely new tourist segments. The advantages of the parallel entry model are also evident in the possibilities of joint advertising, i.e. advertising at the level of the host destination. The reach of such advertising is larger and wider in the global tourism market, and the cost of unity is lower. The model of parallel market entry is also recommended when introducing a modified (improved) specialised tourism product, as it strengthens the impression of originality of the previous content. The attention of tourists is attracted to different contents of one destination at the same time, so some of them will perceive the modified contents that existed earlier as something completely new and will be more attractive to them (adapted from Pride & Ferrell, 2000; Rocco & Hodak, 2013).

- Ad3) If the tourism company already has a loyal customer base, it is not necessary to rush this phase. A later market entry model is recommended. Promotional activities reinforce interest in the new offer that is being provided. The gradual announcement of new specialised tourist content stimulates the interest of the wider tourist public as well. The previous experience and the market image of the tourist entity discourage competitors from offering their own imitations of the announced content. In the author's practice, the model of later market entry has had a positive effect on the lifespan of a new specialised tourism product (Šerić, 2004, 2008; Šerić, Pavlinović, et al., 2011). Additional argumentation for choosing a later market entry model and maintaining the attention of the loyal tourist clientele. Gradual introduction of new content while removing some existing content from the offer causes tourists to continuously monitor the assortment of such tourist facilities. In the author's practice related to the business with sales intermediaries (travel agencies), the trend of faster acceptance of new content as a replacement for content removed from the offer of the same company was confirmed.

In addition to deciding on a marketing model, the tourism company should also simultaneously decide on which outbound markets to place the new offer. With each new offer, the public's attention is additionally drawn to the tourist facility making that offer. However, each emission market also means personalised advertising for a new, specialised tourism product. Outbound markets, which are intended to stimulate greater interest of the tourist public in the overall offer of the subject, are to be given priority. Such advertising requires not only that the tourist audience be informed about the new offer but also about the environment in which it is offered (destination with other attractions and resources). This implies higher advertising costs (presence at tourism fairs, special promotions, etc.). All decisions should be aligned with the defined marketing strategy (Chapter 4) and the strategic objectives of developing a new specialised tourism product (Chapter 6).

During the marketing process of a new specialised tourism product, the specifics of the target tourism segments (desires, motives, attitudes, preferences, cultural influences, etc.) are analysed again. Logistical support for commercialisation (promotional and sales activities) is adjusted according to the current findings.

Each new specialised tourism product is first adopted by the innovator group. Innovator tourists today are particularly interested in content based on new technologies. They are tourists who are primarily attracted by new content and new forms of tourist service delivery, which they buy on a trial basis and for which they quickly decide. The intensity of promotional activities does not have a significant impact on the trial purchase of innovators (Lockwood, 2009). It is important that information about new content is available to them. The *perception of something new* may be enough to create the impression that the content of similar specialised tourism products is different (Lidwell et al., 2006). This paradox is a consequence of today's offering of many different categories of specialised tourism products that tourists select based on similar or even identical needs and incentives. This expands the opportunities for developing new content when it is based on known desires and motivations of the tourist population served. In theory, innovators represent only 2.5% of the total potential tourist population (adapted from Kotler et al., 2009). In the author's practice, they have been shown to be younger tourists who are more likely to seek challenges and adventure, have higher levels of education and have better financial status (Prorok et al., 2019).

The tourism segment of *early adopters* is more cautious when *buying* new specialised tourism products *for the first time*. The attention of this segment can be further stimulated by advertising the features of the new offer that might be particularly attractive to them, depending on their age and interests. This segment is characterised by asking for additional information about new content as soon as it is marketed but does not immediately decide to make a *test purchase*. According to the literature, early adopters make up 13.5% of the total structure of the potential tourist population of a broadcast market (adapted according to Kotler et al., 2009). Nowadays, this tourist segment is also characterised by a higher level of education, higher incomes and good information about the tourist offer. Although they are more reluctant to make a *test purchase* decision, their positive comments about the new tourist offer on social networks attract the attention of a larger segment – *the early majority* (Borovac Zekan et al., 2011; Jerkić & Šerić, 2014). According to the literature, this segment is 34% of the total structure of the tourist population of a given market (according to Kotler et al., 2009). The attention of the early majority is further stimulated by the intensification and expansion of promotional activities through various media (Bilandžić, 2008). When deciding to try a new specialised tourist service, they are more cautious than the previously mentioned segments. They decide to make their first purchase based on positive impressions and comments from innovators and early adopters. This segment is dominated by middle-class tourists. They are more cautious about consuming non-board media but have a positive attitude towards new content. In contrast to them, the late majority segment is characterised by scepticism towards new tourist attractions. The author's experience suggests that this segment of tourists generally opts for a test purchase in the later stages of the life cycle of a new product (Šerić & Jurišić, 2015; Šerić, Mihanović, et al., 2020). According to demographic characteristics, this segment is dominated by older tourists with conservative and traditional attitudes (Prorok et al., 2019). It is advisable to focus the advertising intended for this segment on more traditional features of the offer (availability and friendliness of sales representatives, service providers, safety of tourists, etc.). According to the literature, the share of this segment in the tourist population of the broadcast market is also 34% (Kotler et al., 2009). The remaining part of the tourist population is 16%. In the literature, they are called *indecisive* because they decide to make a *test purchase* of a new specialised tourism product when the offer of the destinations that are not on board is modest, the prices are cheap and they receive a discount, etc. (Prorok et al., 2019). These tourists are characterised not only by their traditional attitudes but also by their scepticism towards anything that is a new experience for them. They are also characterised by higher social sensitivity and limited financial resources for non-board consumption (Šerić & Talijančić, 2011). Considering their total share of the broadcasting market, it does not make economic sense to modify certain promotional activities and sales packages specifically for them.

The advertising and logistic support for the sale of a new specialised tourism product on the outbound market is adapted to the target segment of tourists. Generalisation of advertising to a broader potential tourist demand, which requires higher advertising intensity, leads to higher costs. Moreover, such advertising may reduce the impression of originality of the new special tourism product. If *special* advertising activities are planned in the introductory phase, it is advisable to target them to the early adopters, as they are an important lever for the first purchases of the early majority in the market.

In addition to qualitative standards, the interest of tourists in accepting new content is also contributed by the selected sales network with accompanying sales services (Šerić, Dadić, et al., 2020; Šerić, Jakšić Stojanović, et al., 2023). When offering new content to innovators and early adopters, only the qualitative and legal standards of the category of tourist services to which they belong are important. The early majority is additionally encouraged to test the offered alternatives. In the *Stone Lights* project, the early majority was further attracted by the introduction of new lighthouses for tourist accommodation every year. The expansion of additional services in order to create the impression of higher value of a specialised tourism product helps to attract the attention of the late majority in the tourist practice. In the *Stone Lights* project, this was practiced by expanding additional opportunities during the tourist stay in the lighthouse (fishing with the lighthouse keepers, preparation of meals from local ingredients under the guidance of qualified lighthouse keepers, accompanied diving trips, etc.). These additional services were introduced after several years of a standardised offer – a tourist stay in the lighthouse (accommodation without accompanying facilities).

Chapter 9

Brand and Brand Management of the Specialised Tourism Product

A branded specialised tourism product is easier to differentiate in a category, i.e. a niche with similar tourist offers (Šerić, Vitner Marković, et al., 2017). Branding a specialised tourism product with specific characteristics has a positive impact on the umbrella brand of the company that develops it. The brand of a specialised tourism product should summarise information about the special features of the offer. The special features are graphically represented with appropriate symbols. The symbolism should be connected with the content of the offer, to which the brand name, design and colour are adapted. The brand should strengthen the associations with a particular offer.

The characteristics of a tourist entity, i.e. the specifics of a specialised tourism product, are prerequisites for an umbrella *tourist brand* (Šerić, 2014; Šerić, Jerković, et al., 2017; Šerić & Perišić, 2012). The umbrella brand is an important distinguishing feature for a tourist entity. Due to the specificity of tourism, tourists' perception and experience of a tourism brand by tourists depend on many direct and indirect associations (Šerić, Jakšić Stojanović, et al., 2023). Different associations of the brand in the perception of tourists are also a prerequisite for the development of *sub-brands*. In the Stone Lights project, the umbrella brand was developed as an association for tourist stays at the lighthouse, and each lighthouse was promoted as a separate *sub-brand*. The diversity of the natural environment, architectural solutions of the lighthouse, historical stories and legends related to the locality, etc. were used as specific characteristics of each sub-brand. A prerequisite for the effective development of sub-brands is the existence of a recognisable, basic umbrella brand (a tourism brand unit). In the field of specialised tourism products, the tourist unit can develop sub-brands for all content with different characteristics in the existing offer. Since the specifics of the content are the rule in the specialised tourist offer, they form the basis for the development of the sub-brand (Šerić, 2019a).

The recognition value and originality of the brand of a specialised tourism product help to promote the first, *trial purchase* (Šerić, Vitner Marković, et al., 2017). Brand loyalty of a specialised tourism product is promoted and maintained

Specialised Tourism Products, 103–121
Copyright © 2024 Neven Šerić, Ivana Kursan Milaković and Ivan Peronja
Published under exclusive licence by Emerald Publishing Limited
doi:10.1108/978-1-83549-408-020241009

through brand management activities (Šerić, Jakšić Stojanović, et al., 2023). Brand management activities are adapted to the specific behaviours and value measures of the target tourism clientele. The process of adoption or acceptance of a new tourism brand is gradual, as is the process of acceptance of a new specialised tourism product. The acceptance of a tourism brand leads to brand loyalty. A tourist who is loyal to a particular tourism brand identifies with it, i.e. with the market value of the content it represents (Šerić, Ljubica, et al., 2015). The brand of a specialised tourism product also contributes to the intensity of its visibility in the niche in which it is positioned (Šerić & Uglešić, 2014).

Loyalty to the brand of a specialised tourism product is expressed by the tourist's preference in choosing competing content in the same market niche. Loyalty to a particular tourist brand has a positive effect on the selection of a particular content among the characteristics of different offers. Loyalty to a brand is recognised in the market through repeated purchases and the strengthening of loyalty towards the entire tourist offer of the company for which the brand stands. Tourists who are loyal to the brand of a specific offer (content) contribute to the intensity of brand communication and thus to the perception of its market value through repeated purchases and positive comments on social networks. Due to all the mentioned facts, brand management activities are an important part of the commercialisation process of a new specialised tourism product.

9.1. Identity, Recognition and Market Value of the Brand

The brand of a specialised tourism product is positioned in the market through the presence or marketing of branded content. Secondarily, the brand's market position is strengthened through the promotion of brand identity. Brand identity promotion can be effectively carried out by staff engaged in the process of providing a specialised tourism service. In order for such personnel to effectively promote brand identity, they have to *understand* the essence of the brand, accept it and contribute to the *fulfilment of the brand promise* at the level of their responsibility in the process of service delivery. The essence of a brand is its core content. The *brand promise* of a specialised tourism product implies specific associations in the perception of the target tourist population in terms of the quality of the content offered (reliability, safety, added value and longevity).

The brand identity of a specialised tourism product can thus be seen as its core, i.e. the content that the brand represents. Global tourism experiences speak to the need to connect the brand concept to its identity. Exact examples of good tourism practice are destination brands: *100% Pure New Zealand, Edinburgh Inspiring Capital, I Love NY* and the like. In the context of branding a specific tourism product, the experience of integrating resources, natural attractions, cultural heritage, historical artifacts and man-made attractions as part of the identity is useful. Exact examples of such destination brands are *Disney World, Lego Land* and the like.

In the above examples, the brand identity is implemented through the *brand story*. The brand identity of a specialised tourism product represents its essence, the core of brand content usable for marketing management.

The recognisability of the brand of a specialised tourism product requires an impressive and clear identity. The brand promise of a specialty tourism product should be based on realistic assumptions, consistent and unique characteristics of the brand content (*...a tourist stay in a remote lighthouse, the way lighthouse keepers lived with their families a 100 or more years ago*). With the results of several studies, the authors have demonstrated that the identity of a tourism brand, defined by its functional advantages, positively affects tourists' perception of the quality of branded content (Jakšić Stojanović, Janković, Šerić, & Vukilić, 2019; Jakšić Stojanović & Šerić, 2018; Jakšić Stojanović & Šerić, 2019b; Jakšić Stojanović et al., 2020; Jakšić Stojanović, Šerić, et al., 2019; Šerić, 2017; Šerić & Batalić, 2018; Šerić, Ljubica, et al., 2015 and others).

The recognisability of a brand in the perception of tourists is determined by its memorability and the associations it stimulates, by recalling and making tourists aware of the brand and what it represents. In previous decades, the tourism brand was analysed based on the totality of the perceived characteristics of its image. The evaluation of the market value of the brand was neglected. Recently, the attitude towards the brand has changed. A strong positive relationship has been demonstrated between a *strong* brand and the achievement of a higher price for the branded product and indirectly with the impact on the reputation of the tourism entity, i.e. the branded destination (Buhalis & Sinarta, 2019).

The market value of the brand of a specialised tourism product can be estimated based on the attitude of tourists, how much they are willing to pay for the offered content. The current market value of a brand for a specialised tourism product can also be measured by its contribution to *tourists' purchase decision*. The perception of a higher market value of the brand is the assumption of a higher premium on the price. The perception of a high market value of the brand of a specialised tourism product represents a very concrete competitive advantage of brand content. How sustainable this is depends on market trends, new competitive tourism content and maintaining the quality of tourism services. The market value of the brand is a kind of market *strength* and represents the financial and perspective value of the branded content.

Based on the knowledge of the market perception of the brand value, the accompanying advertising mix is also formed (ways and approaches in the communication of the specialised tourism product with the target tourist markets). The market value of the specialised tourism product's brand increases with the growth of tourists' loyalty to certain brand content. This may be a result of growing global familiarity, perception of growing quality of services and strengthening associations with the attractiveness of brand content (Jakšić Stojanović et al., 2019b; Jakšić Stojanović, Janković, Šerić, & Vukilić, 2019).

The measure of the brand value of a specialised tourism product on the target market is the upper limit of the price tourists are willing to pay for the branded content. In business practice, the market value of the brand *is built* by strengthening the recognition of the name, promoting the loyalty of the target tourists, the image of the high quality of the brand and emphasising its associations in all forms of communication with the target tourist markets (Šerić, 2014). The market value of the brand of a specialised tourism product contributes to its added value. This is reflected today in positive comments on social networks for all content that is in line with current global tourism trends.

Tourists' awareness of the brand of a specialised offer is reflected in recognition and intense recall, which today can also be followed on social networks. The associations with the brand are recognised by the perceived characteristics of the brand in the minds of the tourist public.

In business, there is often a dilemma regarding the extent to which the market value of the brand of a specialised tourism product contributes to the company's bottom line. The author's research has shown that analysing only one indicator of the brand value of a specialised tourism product does not provide relevant insight into its long-term market potential (Šerić, 2012b; Šerić & Meža, 2014; Šerić, Pavlinović, et al., 2011; Šerić & Perišić, 2012; Šerić & Talijančić, 2011). Due to the same knowledge of metrics and methods of determining market value, the combination of various financial indicators of brand value is observed. Financial indicators are often based on the analysis of the influence of brand perception on the purchase decision for brand content and the creation of tourist loyalty. By weighting selected financial indicators, it is possible to express the value of the brand in money. Despite its practicality, the weakness of determining the market value of a brand based on various financial indicators lies in the random setting of assumptions. For this reason, the authors tend to use the combined method of measuring the market value of the brand. This can be found in the literature as *Brand Asset Valuator – BAV* (https://www.mbaskool.com/business-concepts/marketing-and-strategy-terms/1859-brand-asset-valuator-bav.html). The approach to measuring the market value of a brand using the *BAV* is based on testing the perception of a brand offering by potential customers by measuring up to 56 indicators of brand value. The indicators are divided into two basic dimensions and four sub-dimensions. To evaluate the market value of a specialised tourism product, the first basic dimension would be the analysis of the brand's reputation with sub-dimensions of the brand's esteem and the level of awareness of its existence among tourists. As the second basic dimension of the brand of a specialised tourism product, its strength would be analysed through the sub-dimensions of differentiation from competing brands and market relevance of the brand content. This approach to evaluating the brand of a specialised tourism product is based on the assumption that its reputation on the market is a consequential indicator that depends on changes in the strength of the brand's influence on its attractiveness to the tourist clientele and stimulates them to make an initial purchase (Šerić, Peronja, et al., 2020).

9.2. Management of the Brand of a Specialised Tourism Product

The actual, real value of the brand of a specialised tourism product is reflected in the competitiveness of the branded content and the loyalty of tourists to it (Šerić, Peronja, et al., 2020). Based on this assumption, brand management activities represent an investment in the assets of the tourist entity rather than a marketing expense. The activities to manage the brand of a specialised tourism product in function are:

- facilitating market understanding of branded content;
- optimising the sale of branded content;
- enhancing the impression of legal protection of the brand;
- perception of high-quality branded content;
- promoting loyalty to branded content;
- enhancing brand differentiation and branded content.

The management of the brand of a specialised tourism product is carried out in practice by highlighting the brand in selected media (which are assumed to be followed by the target tourist audience) and by all other activities that help to recall the brand and strengthen its awareness among the tourist audience. The activities are carefully chosen if they help to reinforce the impression of the brand identity and the specialised tourist brand product. When solving dilemmas related to the set marketing budget, priority should be given to the activities that directly contribute to the differentiation of the brand of a specialised tourism product. Multimedia presentations of the brand and brand content at international tourism trade shows are recommended, as this is where most tourism entities focus on promoting their receptive tourism markets and destinations. Focusing advertising on specialised tourism facilities and their attributes, and linking that advertising to the brand it represents, attracts the attention of the broader tourism audience, especially sales intermediaries. Including a larger number of sales intermediaries in the prospect also has a positive impact on the global visibility of the tourism brand.

When designing and selecting brand management activities, preference should be given to those that can further motivate tourists to make an initial purchase.

Brand management activities should be developed during the process and preparation of a new specialised tourism product for its marketing, and their implementation in practice often begins only after the brand (and the new specialised tourism product) is positioned in a specific market niche.

Considering the peculiarities of tourism as a social phenomenon, managing the brand of a specialised tourism product implies actions aimed at strengthening the perception of its value. In this regard, it is advisable to highlight a specific relationship with a strategic tourist segment (age, nationality, etc.), where it is assumed that the brand is credible for a test purchase of the brand offer. Such an approach implies an identical marketing treatment of the brand and the brand content – aspects of originality, content, quality and promoted value for the tourist. The brand management of a specialised tourism product forms and summarises the combination of the characteristic values of the brand content in a special way. These values should be promoted in such a way that they connect the conscious and intuitive impression of the brand with the tourist target clientele. By transforming the value characteristics of the brand into substantial benefits for the tourist target audience (functional and emotional benefits), the impression of the brand is reinforced by the uniqueness of what it represents.

It should be noted that according to the author's practical experience, the exception to the mentioned *rules* are brands of specialised tourism products, created primarily to stimulate a certain emotion in the target tourist group. In the case of the Stone Lights project, the focus was on emotions of romance in the seclusion of the world, on the special experience of sunrises and sunsets in the specific environment of the offshore islands and on the impression of mysticism of the centuries-old lighthouse buildings.

The management of the brand of a specialised tourism product aimed at specific emotions of the tourist audience is complex, as it involves the simulation of the reactions of the selected tourist audience (Šerić, 2014, 2019b). The management activities of such a marketing-oriented brand should be based more on *fictions* and less on reality. It is about the so-called emotional branding, which in tourism implies postulates of anthropology, expectations, experiences and visions of tourists. Since this topic is not the focus of the book, the interested are referred to Evtushenko (2013) and Selected readings in *Consumer neuroscience & neuro-marketing* (compendium by Ramsey, 2014).

In the modern practice of brand management, the differences between the conservative and modern conceptions are shown by Kotler et al. (2009). Combining the good experience of both concepts in recent tourism practice, it is advisable to base the brand management activities of a specialised tourism product on them:

- suggestions from tourists who have made a *test purchase*;
- consistency of the brand's impression with the test buyers' tourism experience and their impression of meeting the expectations of a specialised tourism product;
- the degree of confidence in the brand of a specialised tourism product in accordance with the quality of provision of a particular service that can be guaranteed;
- improving the quality of a specialised tourism product in order to strengthen preferences for its brand;
- strengthening brand awareness based on the attractiveness of brand content;
- linking the identity with the brand personality of the specialised tourism product;
- transforming the impression of the functionality of brand content into the impression of the usefulness and availability of the offer;
- transforming the presence of the brand of a specialised tourism product in the global tourist market into its proximity to the target tourist clientele;
- transforming the brand communication into a dialogue with the target tourist segments;
- transforming the service of providing specialised tourist content into a specific relationship between tourists and the brand (a prerequisite for building and maintaining tourists' loyalty to the brand).

Brand management activities that help to reinforce positive emotions towards brand content should help to strengthen the trust of the target tourist population in the offer. All the above facts suggest that the focus of the brand of a specialised tourism product should be on a specific emotion.

The findings from the research and practice of the *Stone Lights* project also show that brand content and personnel involved in selling and providing a specialised tourism product (especially lighthouse keepers and ship crews calling at the lighthouse) are useful marketing levers. Contributions to the intensity of brand emotions transfer are defined standards of providing a specialised tourist service but also established rules of behaviour for tourists (in lighthouse tourism, the same consequence is the fact that lighthouses are objects of navigation safety – e.g. it is obligatory to close the windows after sunset so that the light from the apartment does not disturb the light signal of the lighthouse, to pay attention to defined rules for the disposal and removal of waste, reuse of sanitary water in water for irrigation of green areas). Such rules of tourist behaviour represent a concrete standard of the brand of a specialised tourism product in accordance with the sustainable and responsible use of commercialised resources. This also has a positive impact on the business image and reputation of the company offering a specialised tourism product in the global market (Cooper, 2021; Jaffari & Xiao, 2021; Meler & Magaš, 2014; Pineda et al., 2004; Waeaver, 2006 and others).

Brand management of a specialised tourism product requires creativity and innovation. An attractive brand image is built gradually through various media and channels (Kozinets et al., 2010; Pike, 2008; Šerić & Marušić, 2019). The advertising mix within the brand management activities for the specialised tourism product is adapted to the targeted tourist segments (including all advertising messages, slogans and symbols used). The continuity of brand management activities is also important to prevent the advertising campaigns of competitors offering something similar from confusing tourists as to who is offering what and where. To reduce this risk in branding, special attention should be paid to:

- Symbols used to identify the content of the specialised tourist offer (associative power of the logo, predominant colours and graphic shapes).
- Selection of media and advertising messages to achieve the maximum personality of the messages sent (stories, mood, peculiarities of the content, etc.).
- The atmosphere of the impression of a specialised tourist offer (positive feelings, attractiveness and encouragement to buy on trial).
- They select events that promote the brand of a specialised tourism product.
- The image of the brand resulting from the current perception of tourists about the brand content.

It is advisable to base brand management activities for a specialised tourism product on Keller's (2003) brand market value model. Decision-making related to brand management activities involves analysing the behaviour of tourists who often choose non-board facilities, especially those that fall into the category of specialised tourism products. The mentioned model is based on information and experience of tourists about a specialised tourism product. Considering other theoretical postulates, it is advisable to take into account the brand and tourism theme awareness and the current brand image of the specialised tourism product when designing brand management activities. Brand awareness is based on the recognition and recall of the brand by tourists. Brand image represents the tourists' perception of the brand content. The perception of the brand can be analysed through its associations in the tourist's subconscious. Associations as elements of the brand image of a special tourism product determine three characteristics:

(1) brand strength;
(2) brand preferences;
(3) brand uniqueness.

Following Keller's model (2003), the brand of a special tourism product will achieve a higher market value the better known it is on the market, the stronger and more desirable the positive associations with it are, and the more extraordinary the brand content is.

In this sense, it can be concluded that the strategic objective of managing the brand of a special tourism product is to strengthen the *visibility* and *perceptibility* of the brand content in the market. It should be remembered that the quality of the brand offer and the experience of the tourist entity are not sufficient to maintain the market share achieved if they are not sufficiently visible to the target market segments. Maintaining the visibility of the brand and brand content depends on the originality and intensity of promotional activities. They also help strengthen the positive image of the brand and align this image with the values and personalities of the target tourism clientele (strategic tourism segment). Activities to maintain and strengthen the credibility of the brand also contribute to a positive brand image. All of the above should be taken into account when designing an advertising mix that carries the brand of a specialised tourism product. The activities should emphasise the added value and uniqueness of the brand content. The author's research results have shown that it is more efficient to emphasise several simple features of the brand content than one complex basic feature. The dilemma to think about is related to committing to a particular advertising strategy. When the competitive strengths and advantages of brand content are clear, it is possible to evaluate the impact of each activity to manage the brand of a specialised tourism product. In this way, it is possible to decide on brand management activities that contribute to maintaining and strengthening the target image depending on the growth of sales of specialised tourism products.

Regardless of the initial reactions of tourists, who belong to the category of *innovators*, it is only after the commercialisation of the specialised tourism product that the real *market story* begins, in which all the lessons learned from the previous stages of the development of the new tourist content should be used.

Whether its life cycle curve resembles the theoretical curve will be seen in the future.

Research by the authors (Šerić, 2012a; Šerić & Luković, 2010, 2013; Šerić, Pavlinović, et al., 2011; Šerić & Perišić, 2012; Šerić et al., 2012; Šerić & Talijančić, 2011) shows deviations from the theoretical curve of the life cycle for specialised tourism products. The reasons for the deviation are often the narrower segments of tourists who choose such offers, the susceptibility of demand to tourism trends and whims and more (Prorok et al., 2019). Consequently, when advertising, it is important to find the right triggers for the target tourist group and, over time, change the content of the offer and alter the *triggers* to encourage them to buy, similar to the scenario when the existing tourist offer is additionally adapted to the emerging tourism market (Šerić & Marušić, 2019). For this reason, test marketing and market testing are recommended activities even after the commercialisation of a new specialised tourism product, and the model of *later market entry* as a general decision in the commercialisation of a specialised tourism product is imposed as a lower risk alternative.

In the author's practice, the decision to launch a specialised tourism product later quickly turned into an exponential phase of sales growth thanks to a thorough marketing preparation. This phase would last until the tourist segments originally targeted were covered. A maturation phase followed, supported by modifications to the original offer. Changes were made to make the already positioned specialised tourism product attractive to some other tourist segments. Such an approach would lead to additional revenue growth as the loyalty of the already attracted segments was not lost. In the later stages of the life cycle, demand was maintained through additions and additional changes to the core content.

Considering all that has been said in this chapter, the question arises when it is time to remove a specialised tourism product from the market. One of the indicators is when the brand of a specialised tourism product reaches the graveyard zone. But even then, there are opportunities for additional modifications to the basic and additional content, which opens up the possibility of *rejuvenation*. It is time for rejuvenation in the project *Stone Lights* – a specialised tourism product – a stay at the Adriatic lighthouses, so in the following chapter, a practical business case of the implementation of the theory of the previous chapters is presented.

Case Study 6: *Dark Tourism*

Dark *tourism represents one of the contemporary tourism phenomena. The global dark tourism case studies show some possibilities of commercialisation of such contents: Hiroshima, Nagasaki and Aogikahara (Japan), the World Trade Centre (USA), Pompeii and the ridge of the Costa Concordia (Italia), working camps (Russia) and camp Auschwitz (Germany). This offer is often conceptually associated with the legal inconsistency of tourism because it is based on some kind of human suffering. On the other side, interest for dark tourism offer is growing. Today, such contents could be included as a part of the regular tourist arrangements if they exist on the receptive market. The dark tourism is developing often on the historical*

(*Continued*)

(Continued)

resources. Because of that, it cannot be said that this is a totally new form of specialised tourist offer. The first research of dark tourism was during the 70s of the 20th century but systematically analysed during the 90s of the 20th century (Stone, 2013). Dark tourism could be defined as a systematic integration of travel tourism through places associated by death, tragedy and people suffering (Tarlow, 2005).

The main argument for the development of dark tourism offer is the all-year potential and possibility of tourist's independence towards bad weather conditions (Joly, 2010). Despite the contribution to the differentiation and competitiveness of the offer, the potential resources for the development of dark tourist facilities are still often neglected. This is a consequence of insufficient knowledge of the development of specialised tourism products. In the dark tourism offer, a particular problem refers to sociocultural and thanatological repercussions that this offer makes sensitive to the ethical standards of the public. The result could be negative publicity for the whole touristic destination. Due to such risks, despite the growing global interest in the dark tourism, these offers are slowly developing. In attempting to clear up some doubts, as well as positive and negative experiences in global tourism practice, the authors carried out findings of several researches and offered a framework model for creating a dark tourist product with recommended variables of significant impact.

Places of natural disasters, history military conflicts, mass murders, terrorist attacks and cemeteries (where buried popular persons) are fuelling the growth in visits of individuals and tourist groups. Such contents through the marketing representation could attempt tourist interests. Concentration camps (World War II) were attracting millions of tourists through past decades (Filipović, 2017; Rašetina, 2010).

Dark tourism offer needs to be based on rare and unusual resources nowadays (Hosany et al., 2007; Kladou & Kehagias, 2014; Stone, 2006; Tarlow, 2005). Dark tourism offer is based on content related to accidents, deaths and other kind of people's suffering (Sharpley & Stone, 2009). The potential of dark tourism is reflected in the multidimensionality of motivation. The optimisation of dark tourist product assumes systematic development and management throughout the life cycle. The implementation of dark content in an destination offer implies a commitment to a particular category – dark thematic, dark matter exhibitions, dungeons and penitentiaries, cemeteries, places of military conflicts, concentration camps, etc. (Stone, 2006). Marketing dilemmas need to be clarified in the context of the defined future vision of the destination. Development of isolated dark tourism content can result in its domination and unobtrusive image of whole destination, which is not rational if there are other resources for the development of other specialised tourism products.

Focus in author's research of dark tourism resources was on Dalmatia, the part of the Republic of Croatia. Authors extract potential variables and offer the model for the marketing practice. Analysing the modest theoretical opus of the developmental concepts of specialised tourism products, the variables are recognised between knowingly created attractions and the promotion of experiences that are interpreted. The relevant component of the dark tourism story is an expected range of tourist interests about some people's sufferings (Stone, 2013). The starting points in the author's research are defined according to Stone model (2006).

Some other authors (Angelevska Najdeska & Rakicevik, 2012; Bieger, 2000; Bigne et al., 2001; Tsung Hung, 2013; Vargas-Sanchez et al., 2011) warn that creating specialised tourist products need to be in accordance with the standards of sustainable tourism development. The particular attention needs to be paid to the access to the commercialisation of links between the past and the present (relationship between the former victims and their present descendants and tourists). In the conceptualisation of relations between localities and the resources of the development of dark tourist offer, it is advisable to add the heterotopic standard (Stone, 2013). It warns of the need to know the critical level of social acceptance of particular content. The sites of dark tourism content are often places of contradiction and division. Sometimes, these places can cause intensified significance for former residents. Because of that, some restrictions on the intensity of a tourist visit should be defined. Ethical and moral standards, media and promotional implications and issues of political interpretation of content on which the dark tourist product is based should be taken into account (Aas et al., 2005; Armenski et al., 2012; Edgell et al., 2008; Vargas-Sanchez et al., 2011). The political dimension in interpretation of such contents of the past has an impact on collective consciousness. Because of that, the dilemma of the ethical correctness should be in mind. Many stated authors point to the need of regulating the standards of tourist behaviour because of potential sociocultural problems. It is advisable to evaluate the role and potential of dark tourism in the wider secularisation of society (sadness and traumas).

The findings of the author's research indicate that many of existing dark tourism products are not systematically designed but have been identified as resources for attracting the attention of certain tourist segments. Commercialisation of potential dark resources sometimes does not have the characteristics of a specialised tourist product because the marketing potential of developing and managing their commercialisation is neglected. This is important because the implementation of marketing increases attractiveness and competitiveness of each touristic offer (Crouch, 2007; Dwyer et al., 2004). The interest for visiting dark tourism places could be encouraged by the media. The long-term and efficient valorisation of these places sometimes the guerrilla marketing activities are important key (the story on which some content is based).

It is difficult to find concrete explanations for the attraction of dark content. This could be recognised by neuro marketing research. The media sensationalism encourages public condemnation, and negative connotations are possible with tourists who visit these places independently. If these contents are being offered as a part of the integrated destination product, the public condemnation of the visitors could be transmitted to the organisers of such travels. That results in a simpler decision-making of potential interests for visits to such places. The content of a disaster and human suffering links the creation of a tourist story that promotes specific emotional reactions of visitors to the tour programme. Dark tendencies encourage visitor's fears, even though the same was not done

(Continued)

(*Continued*)

consciously. Detailed historical foundation, educational meaning and authenticity of the location are identified as exploitable variables of transformation of potential dark *resources into the* dark *tourist product. The potential of technological and sociocultural factors should be emphasised as these can significantly contribute to the attractiveness of the* dark *tourist offer. Technological factors contribute to the public's awareness of* dark *content and sociocultural contributions to the social acceptability of such tourist contents.*

The vision of a dark tourism offer should be aligned with the nearby destinations and strategy of the tourism development. Secularisation and individualisation, together with weakening religious influences in the public, simplifies the definition of moral frameworks in the commercialisation of the dark tourism offer. Promotions of such content contribute to the media and could create a state of moral panic (Seaton & Lennon, 2004). This is the result of moral debates. Since moral panic is one of the symptoms, but not the consequence of dark *tourism, the potential of marketing in the development and management of such tourism products is evident*

The territory of Dalmatia in the Republic of Croatia has historically been characterised by the frequent migrations of the population and military conflicts on land and on the sea, as evidenced by many historical artifacts, as well as many tourist exploitable stories and legends (Hitrec, 2012). Findings of authors research conducted have pointed some limitations and opportunities for the development of the dark *tourism offer.*

Fundamental constraints are required financial resources for the development of such specialised offer and the lack of professional staff for the creation and management of the same, the need for modification of the destination promotion in which dark tourist offer would be given (the complexity of the implementation of the dark tourism offer into an integrated destination product – split attitudes), the modest interest of local tourist stakeholders for marketing investments in dark *tourism and the division of attitudes of the local population with regard to historical events.*

Possibilities are opening of the new emission tourist markets, adapting potential dark *contents in higher levels for tourist consumption, contributing of the* dark *content to the preservation of neglected heritage and identity constituents, the growth of the entire tourist visit, networking of various local entities into an integrated tourist offer, encouraging additional education of local tourist staff (summer or winter tourism), long-term sustainable positioning of the integrated destination offer.*

Research findings have confirmed that the offer of dark *tourism is appealing to most tourist segments, since no segment has been identified among the respondents who, due to ethical or other prejudices, would not visit such places in Dalmatia. The introduction of such tourist facilities would increase the tourist season. The investments for the development of* dark *tourism products are economically rational due to the high rate of return and the higher differentiation and competitiveness of the destination.*

The recommended model for creating a dark *tourism product towards findings of author's research is shown in Fig. 6.*

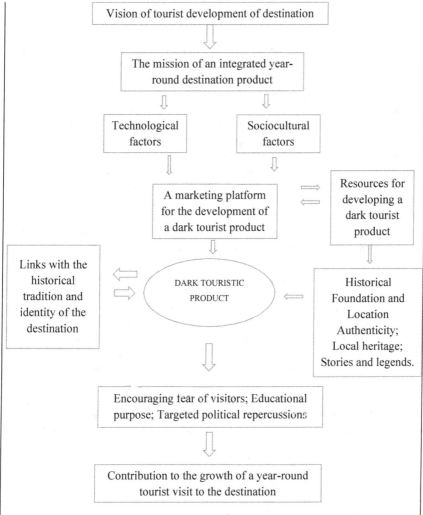

Fig. 6.   A Recommended Model for Creating a Dark Tourist Product. *Source:* Adapted from: Šerić, Mihanović, et al. (2020).

The findings of this research confirm the importance of dark *tourist content to the differentiation, competitiveness and the growth of all-year visit. Still in the global tourism practice of developing and managing dark tourism offer mismatch with some receptive components is overwhelmingly focused on* dark *content. Neglect of sociocultural issues makes the dark tourism offer vulnerable to the ethical standards of the public. Consequently, frequent condemnation of a part of the public by both interested tourists and travel organisers including such*

(Continued)

(Continued)

contents is in their arrangements. The development of a sustainable competitive integrated destination tourism product implies the valorisation of all potentially usable resources. Sustainable tourism development presupposes the systematic development of all specialised tourist products, even the dark tourism offer. Each category of a specialised tourism product is based on certain influential variables. In the case of a dark tourism product, these variables are: historical foundations, location authenticity and local heritage. Technological and sociocultural factors could be helpful in order to reduce the risk of negative publicity of the commercialisation of dark tourist contents. The variable of historical traditions and the identity of the destination show a useful return link with the dark tourism product. It is important to establish the dark tourist contents in the vision and destination mission within which they are offered. All these variables are rationally linked through the marketing platform to ultimately result in dark tourist content by stimulating fear and educating visitors to targeted political repercussions related to the interpretation of dark tourist content. The dark tourism offer can ensure the growth of all-year tourist destination visit. Creating of a dark tourist product should respect victims and respect for current sociocultural criteria. Through such kind of commercialisation of dark tourism, these contents will not be only the silent witnesses and hostages of the past. Systematic management of a dark tourism product can contribute to the reconciliation of people and the creation of a new image of the local and national communities and promotes multiculturalism, understanding and development of good neighbourly relations based on people's association. Dark tourism is an incentive factor for new financial investments, so additional education of tourist staff and encouragement of new motives for travel and visits are needed. However, a systematic approach to developing and managing dark tourism products is necessary by considering variables of influence in the presented model.

Case Study 7: *Solo Female Travel*

Female travel has become a significant phenomenon in the last few years, showing an increment of 88% and indicating a massive cultural shift (Condor, 2023) and explosive growth in the travel industry (Bond, 2023). Some studies (Solo Female Travelers, 2022; Williams, 2023) have found that more than 70% of travellers travel solo, dominantly female, whereas this trend is growing exponentially among women. Concerning gender, 64% of travellers worldwide are female, and only 36% are male (Condor, 2023). In addition, solo female travel, that is, women who travel alone, is a growing trend expected to account for 125 billion dollars in the current year (Condor, 2023).

Here are some information concerning solo female travellers (Condor, 2023):

- *Solo female travel includes different ages. Forty-six per cent of them are aged between 25 and 39. Eighty-one per cent of female travellers are over 45 years old. The most tremendous increase in solo female travel in 2022 came from women aged 65 and older.*
- *Solo female travellers widely use social media (e.g. Instagram and Pinterest).*
- *Travel companies serving solo female travellers have increased by 230% in recent years.*
- *Fifty-nine per cent of solo female travellers intend to travel alone in the next 12 months.*
- *Seventy-five per cent of individuals who choose adventure, culture or nature trips are women.*
- *Fifty-four per cent of solo female travellers recommend Europe for their first solo trip.*

Women are authentic travel influencers. Around 80% of all travel decisions are made by women (Bond, 2023; Williams, 2023). Namely, they make most of the travel bookings for others and account for 70% of the hotel website visits (Solo Female Travelers, 2022). Hence, it is crucial for companies to build trust concerning their roles of being vital decision-makers. Since many tourism agents need help understanding the motivation concerning female solo travel (Solo Female Travelers, 2022), this specialised area is neglected, underexplored, yet interesting and propulsive.

9.2.1. Solo Female Travel Motivation

Women are motivated to travel alone by many factors. Solo female travelling came into focus, particularly after the pandemic, when people wanted to compensate for the lost time (Nath, 2023). Some women cherish solo travel's flexibility and freedom (Solo Female Travelers, 2022). Others see solo travel as an escape from daily routine and responsibilities (Condor, 2023), relaxing, self-care and enjoying 'me-time' (Solo Female Travelers, 2022). Furthermore, many women travel solo for the history, beautiful sceneries, cultural immersion, education, adventure, inspiration-seeking and experiences (Condor, 2023; Unearth Women, 2023; Williams, 2023). Some travel for wellness and mindfulness, while others prefer sustainable travels, 'digital detox' and voluntourism (Unearth Women, 2023). Women travel alone because they want to and because, in this way, they try to challenge themselves. It is not necessarily a lifestyle (Bond, 2023; Solo Female Travelers, 2022). Besides empowerment, solo female travel has some other benefits, such as the exit from the comfort zone, work on a 'good self-ishness', socialisation (new friends and like-minded people), self-introspections and freedom from social expectations. Besides freedom and flexibility, Hosseini et al. (2022) stress the importance of personal factors for a solo female travelling like self-empowerment, independence, exploration and well-being. This trend is also visible in some patriarchal societies, such as Muslim countries (Hosseini et al., 2022; Nikjoo et al., 2021), indicating social change.

According to Condor (2023), the potential reasons stopping females from travelling alone are safety perceptions, getting lost and not feeling alone. Therefore, while travelling alone, women pay attention to safety by regularly communicating and sharing itineraries with their friends and family and staying at trusted hotels. Other reasons for not travelling alone encompass higher costs of solo travel, nobody to share the experience with, feeling guilty about leaving family behind and not having the permission of family to travel alone (Solo Female Travelers, 2022). In addition, in Asian culture, resistance is seen as a barrier to travelling alone. Namely, Asian women travellers need to resist sociocultural expectations for Asian women and sexualised male attention; however, these factors do not discourage them from planning some future solo trips (Seow & Brown, 2018). Considering safety, some women try their first solo trip within a group tour (Nath, 2023). Another trend emerges when women quit their jobs and travel the world (Williams, 2023).

9.2.2. Choosing the Destination

Solo female travellers mainly trust other solo travellers on social networks, i.e. Facebook and online review sites (Solo Female Travelers, 2022). Concerning most desired destinations, Japan is the best place for solo female travellers (Condor, 2023; Williams, 2023). Other top safest destinations are Canada, Finland, New Zealand, Switzerland, Belgium, Iceland, Austria, Uruguay and Chile (Condor, 2023). According to Williams (2023), the top safest countries in the world are Iceland, New Zealand, Denmark, Portugal and Slovenia. The fastest-growing female-friendly destinations are India, Italy and Sri Lanka (Condor, 2023). According to other insights (e.g. Solo Female Travelers, 2022), the United Kingdom and Spain have outranked Italy, whereas Greece is decreasing on the destination selection list. Some US solo female travellers choose additionally intriguing destinations, e.g. Mackinac Island – Great Lakes, Nova Scotia, Charleston (Nath, 2023).

Furthermore, when choosing the destination, women consider various factors. Most of them select due to the cultural attractions, beauty of a destination, safety, local cuisine, and friendliness of the local people, good weather and the country's reputation (Solo Female Travelers, 2022). For more than half of solo female travellers, affordability plays a role, as well as the prices offered by a travel provider, the provider's environmental care and social responsibility and local business ownership (Solo Female Travelers, 2022). In addition, some other aspects are unimportant, such as a presentation on Instagram and language knowledgeability (Solo Female Travelers, 2022).

Moreover, women collectively have 15 trillion dollars and usually spend more than men when travelling, which is essential from the perspective of drivers in the travel industry (Williams, 2023). Concerning all previous insights, we assume that solo female travel will only grow with the current driving factors persisting and with a possibility of some new motives yet to be revealed.

9.3. Social Media and Tourism Branding

Social media includes internet-based services that enable users to create and share content, e.g. photos, links and videos, while using their computers or mobile phones (GlobalData, 2023). Social media refers to different online platforms, such as Instagram, Facebook, X, YouTube, Pinterest, Reddit and WhatsApp (GlobalData, 2023). The fast and extensive expansion in information and communication technology has impacted the global tourism sector over the past decade (Islam, 2021). Moreover, consumer behaviour in tourism is usually driven by the growth of ICT (Buhalis & Law, 2008). This enabled consumers, i.e. travellers, to rely on social media, e.g. blogs, videos, social networks, content communities and other digital media, in all phases of planning their trips. In contrast, tourism agents use social media for promotion, communication and research (Islam, 2021). By becoming an integral part of lives, social media are inevitable in the decision-making process concerning tourism activity (Karaca & Polat, 2022). In addition, the burst of social media platforms, with billions of users actively engaging every day, in the past two decades has connected people and opened a way for social media marketing (Brandt, 2023; Volkman, 2022).

Here are some facts and figures that describe the relationship between social media platforms and the travel industry (Mize, 2022):

- Eighty-five per cent of Millennials use social media platforms to plan their vacation.
- Forty-three per cent of Millennials will not go on a trip if their followers will not be able to see their vacation.
- Thirty-four per cent of them booked a hotel because they saw it on social media via user-generated content.
- Seventy-four per cent of travellers use social media while on vacation.

Furthermore, social media has become an integral part of tourism companies. Namely, companies used social media for their operations during the pandemic, and social media consumption heavily increased by more than 70% (Mize, 2022). Concerning social networks and engagement, market insights (Mize, 2022) indicate that Instagram is highly popular in the travel industry, followed by Twitter, i.e. X, TikTok and Facebook. Given the nature of TikTok, the insights show that this social network represents a very lucrative channel. Moreover, all tourism participants can use social media platforms, particularly social networks, for free, enhancing the opportunities available through such media. An additional important aspect of social media and networks is the opportunity for engagement and interaction.

9.3.1. Social Media Benefits

Social media have brought new experiences to consumers, i.e. tourists. Namely, social media enables consumers, i.e. tourists, to access information regarding the destinations and accompanying content and helps increase the awareness and recognition of tourism aspects and destinations. Studies indicate that tourists are more prone to rely on social media when making travel plans (Wang & Yan, 2022). Scholars (e.g., Dedeoğlu et al., 2020) claim that the Internet and social media platforms are the leading information channels for travel information.

In addition, social media positively influences the tourism industry regarding exposure and reach. In contrast, destinations and businesses gain significant exposure and reach by showing their culture, attractions, and experiences to global audiences (Brandt, 2023). Moreover, social media enables consumers to enhance their active engagement due to its nature, i.e. real-time communication. They also nurture digital influencer partnerships that occur as strategic approaches. Specifically, by collaborating with digital influencers, tourism companies and agents can expose their authenticity and storytelling (Brandt, 2023).

Furthermore, the user, i.e. consumer/traveller-generated content, i.e. content made by the people, not companies, also serves the function of informing and branding communications by generating and sharing the content tourists brand directly and indirectly (Dedeoğlu et al., 2020). Hence, tourism companies and agents need to comprehend social media's and user-generated content's impact on purchasing decisions. In addition, when backed up with tourism influencers, the destination can gain popularity since the destination symbolism takes part by changing tourists' attitudes (Morand et al., 2021). Now, individuals organically share their experiences, i.e. vacation photos, stories and reviews about the destination, hotels and restaurants, making social media an excellent polygon for travel inspiration and planning (Volkman, 2022).

Concerning the digital nomads, travel influencers belonging to Millennials and European Millennials account for a significant share of all expenditures within the tourism industry; it can be said that almost 75% of all European Millennials research trips online, particularly on social media while paying attention to authentic and genuine content (CBI, 2023). In addition, Millennials are highly likely to find brands and services through vlogs, blogs and celebrity endorsements; hence, monitoring their behaviour, e.g. their opinions and what they communicate on their social media channels, is highly recommended (CBI, 2023).

Furthermore, social media is seen as a source for assessing the travellers' needs and motives, decision-making process and travel recommendations (Cheng & Edwards, 2015), particularly given the availability and easiness of devices, e.g. smartphones. Social media plays a vital role in destination branding since it can ease the interaction between tourists, increase the speed of information dissemination and share experiences while enabling the customisation and personalisation of the offers (Brandt, 2023; Hadianfar, 2021). Studies show that social media marketing effectively cultivates tourism marketing to build destination brand equity (Hadianfar, 2021). It can be assumed that social media has essential implications for destination brand equity, consumer/traveller behaviour and managers within the tourism industry. In addition, social media sharing is essential for destination brand awareness (Dedeoğlu et al., 2020).

Studies show that the quality of social media information positively influences travel intention and self-congruity, i.e. the self-image of tourists (Wang & Yan, 2022). Namely, social media has enhanced tourist's ability to obtain information and knowledge about destinations and tourism products and services (Wang & Yan, 2022). Moreover, social media contributes to information sharing and exchange; it can decrease the uncertainty and increase the sense of belonging (Wang & Yan, 2022). Besides, particular emphasis is put on the quality of tourism information on social media, i.e. how useful the information is, particularly one generated by the users, i.e. tourists (Yeap et al., 2014). In addition, content cues of quality of information positively influence destination brand awareness (Ghorbanzadeh et al., 2022).

9.3.2. Social Media and Specialised Tourism Products

While the research on social media and branding recently gained popularity, there is still space concerning specialised tourism products, and such studies still need to keep up with occurrences in different industries (Moro & Rita, 2018). Specialised tourism product niches, i.e. special interests in tourism, are growing and will continue expanding (Stainton, 2023). However, scientific insights into this field are scarce, particularly from the social media perspective. Namely, the existing literature indicates that the most studied aspects concerning social media and tourism included social engagement, smart tourism, nature and tourism experiences and emotional and cultural tourism (Idbenssi et al., 2023), while insignificant attention was given to specialised tourism products in general and from the social media perspective. In addition, several studies have explored city and destination branding, but research on social media and branding still needs to be done (Tran & Rudolf, 2022). Hence, such studies, including digital technologies in the travel industry, are yet to come (Tran & Rudolf, 2022).

Therefore, special attention should be paid to specialised products besides basic content. Namely, the Mediterranean area has many opportunities in this regard. Take, for example, Croatia and lighthouses, then Dubrovnik as a place for Game of Thrones... The main point is to better and more frequently utilise different social media channels to advertise and share content that appeals to specialised tourism products. We believe that a lot needs to be done in this regard, not only by the tourism agents but also tourists.

Thus, it can be concluded that social media has dramatically changed the tourism industry. Social media has become a powerful tool not only for tourists but also for tourism companies. It enables an easy and valuable quality information exchange that drives the tourists' motives and travel planning. It can be assumed that social media will at least remain stable, if not rapidly growing, in drawing the attention of tourists and companies while enhancing the brand awareness of destinations. Future studies should strengthen the exploration of social media's relevance for specialised tourism products.

Chapter 10

Development and Management of a Specialised Tourism Product: *Stay at the Adriatic Lighthouses*

In the 19th century, Austria-Hungary created a valuable resource in the architectural and cultural–historical sense with the project of building a lighthouse in the Eastern Adriatic (Jakšić Stojanović & Šerić, 2018). Each lighthouse building is designed differently. The towers of the lighthouses also differ from each other (Šerić, 2004). Lighthouses have thus become recognisable destination symbols of the places where they were built in this water area (Jakšić Stojanović & Šerić, 2018). Each Adriatic lighthouse has a recognisable identity in a particular place. Naval battles and other historical events took place in the surrounding water area. In the past two decades, many stories and legends have been associated with each lighthouse. The attitude of national political elites and local people towards cultural and historical heritage shows the level of civilisational development of the country (Buhalis, 2000). On the other hand, national cultural and historical heritage can be used for marketing to promote a receptive tourism country (Morrison, 2013). Historical heritage contributes to the recognisability of a tourism country's image and stimulates tourists' interest in visiting (Kušen, 2002). Cultural and historical heritage can be used to develop special tourism products (Šerić & Jurišić, 2014). Responsible and sustainable use of national cultural and historical heritage allows the tourism country to present itself on the global tourism market in an original way. Specialised tourism facilities based on cultural and historical heritage are also a useful feature for differentiating the national tourism offer. Navigating the Adriatic at night, guided by the light signals of the lighthouses, is a unique experience for sailors even today.

The political environment in the water area where Austria-Hungary erected lighthouses 200 years ago was changing. Lighthouses and the tradition of lighthouse keeping are a constant, and today, they are a marketing feature and a recognisable icon of the destination. The project of tourism marketing of the *Stone Lights* represents one of the ways of sustainable and responsible enhancement of cultural and historical heritage to strengthen the competitiveness of the

Specialised Tourism Products, 123–137
Copyright © 2024 Neven Šerić, Ivana Kursan Milaković and Ivan Peronja
Published under exclusive licence by Emerald Publishing Limited
doi:10.1108/978-1-83549-408-020241010

national tourism offer. The design and development of specialised tourism products based on cultural and historical content requires certain standards of sustainable marketing in order to preserve the monumental heritage for future generations (Šerić & Talijančić, 2011).

10.1. Premises of the Idea of Lighthouse Tourism in the Waters of the Eastern Adriatic Sea

In the global tourism market, a growing trend of demand for cultural and his-torical heritage content (Šerić & Talijančić, 2011), ecological environments of preserved landscapes and offering original gastronomic tradition (Prorok et al., 2019) can be observed in the last two decades. Many receptive tourism countries use cultural–historical heritage and ecologically preserved areas to promote the national tourism product. In the practice of national promotion, these features are generalised as information is sent to the general tourist population.

When promoting a specialised tourism product, the focus of market commu-nication should be on narrower segments in special interest niches (Šerić & Jurišić, 2015; Šerić et al., 2014). Recent research on tourist behaviour shows that the number of guests visiting cultural and historical monuments during their stay is increasing (Prorok et al., 2019; Šerić & Talijančić, 2011). The potential of these destination facilities is evident in their usefulness in attracting tourists during off-peak periods. The more frequent promotion of historical heritage in films and television series also contributes to its appeal. Film directors are increasingly looking for destinations with indigenous historic architecture.

Full tourism exploitation of existing resources is achieved by developing a range of specialised tourism products based on these resources. The broader context of the content makes the destination resources attractive to the broader tourist population. The indigenous characteristics of the specialised tourism products allow for a higher premium on prices. Ultimately, such facilities help extend the destination's tourism season.

Despite these facts, many post-transition countries only *sporadically* transform indigenous resources into specialised tourism products and attractions (Prorok et al., 2019). The focus of their tourism development is mainly on accommodation infrastructure. Neglecting differentiated specialised tourism products is the path to mass tourism, which today is neither ecologically nor economically justified. Because of this risk, more intensive training is needed for all those working in tourism to develop and manage specialised tourism products. In addition, it is necessary to identify the resources that can be used for the development of spe-cialised tourism products and to carry out an analysis of their long-term sus-tainable exploitation. Then it is possible to decide on the merits and arguments of the models of commercialisation of resources that can be used for the develop-ment of specialised tourism products for selected tourism segments. This is fol-lowed by the development of such new tourism content and its marketing integration into the tourism offer of the destination and the country.

In managing tourism development in post-transition countries, the necessary synergy and interaction between tourism stakeholders and local government units is often neglected. Examples of cross-border tourism cooperation aimed at joint positioning of specialised tourism products on the world market are rare, although the European Union promotes and finances such tourism development projects.

Cultural and historical heritage is an important feature of national identity and a usable resource for the development of specialised tourism products (Becken, 2005; Buhalis, 2000; Kušen, 2002; Šerić, 2004; Šerić & Talijančić, 2011). A country's tourism image in the global environment depends on the characteristics that define its national resources (Beeton, 2006). Cultural and historical heritage, preserved landscapes and traditional gastronomy can be used in *co-branding* to reposition the destination (Šerić, Jakšić Stojanović, et al., 2023). The tourism appeal of small post-transition countries in the global tourism market is often the result of a recognisable identity (Buhalis, 2000). The recognisable identity of a receptive tourism country has a positive impact on the perception of the value of all tourism products and services (Hedin et al., 2011). Ignoring these facts, the tourism economy becomes focused on mass tourism (Solow, 2008). In the late 1990s, the author's commitment to the tourism enhancement of the lighthouse heritage is a consequence of the desire to show the national tourist public that there is an alternative to mass tourism, which has become the rule of thumb for managing tourism development on the eastern Adriatic coast.

In the Mediterranean, the first *lighthouses* were built as early as 300 years before Christ (Jakšić Stojanović & Šerić, 2018). In the Eastern Adriatic, many preserved lighthouses were built by Austria-Hungary in the 19th century. The lighthouses were built because of the large number of islands, islets and rocks that prevented safe navigation at night. More than 1,200 islands, islets and rocks in the waters of the Republic of Croatia alone made night navigation very risky under complex hydrometeorological conditions (Šerić, 2004). Austria-Hungary financed the construction of the lighthouse primarily for reasons of navigational safety. Forty-eight lighthouse buildings with towers have been preserved on the Croatian part of the Adriatic from the period of lighthouse construction in the 19th century. They were built in the period from 1818 (Savudrija lighthouse in Istria) to 1899 (Three Sisters lighthouse in Rivanjska in the Zadar archipelago). The locations of the lighthouses were chosen in such a way that the range of the light beam connects the main coastal and offshore navigation corridors. The network of navigation corridors is designed so that the maximum visibility of the light cones of adjacent lighthouses is up to 30 nautical miles. The height of the lighthouses was determined according to the location and relief of the surrounding area. These facilities form the basis of the lighthouse heritage, thanks to which lighthouse tourism has developed.

10.2. Lighthouses as Recognisable Destination Icons

The recognition value of lighthouses, mainly thanks to the original architectural solutions with high stone towers and lights, made them specific destination symbols decades before the concept of tourist accommodation on lighthouses was developed. Resources considered to have the potential for tourism content and destination development should be legally protected (from damage to existing architectural and landscape views). Since lighthouses on the Adriatic have been important objects for the safety of navigation since their construction until today, there was no lack of legal protection provided by the declaration of these buildings as cultural and historical heritage in the second half of the 20th century. However, until the end of the 19th century, there was no unified thinking among the general public about the possibilities of tourism valorisation of these resources.

On the other hand, recognisable destination icons, especially those based on cultural and historical heritage, can achieve *cult status*, as evidenced by the UNESCO heritage in tourist destinations. Nowadays, promotional activities in literature, film and other media contribute to this. Famous people (athletes, actors, musicians) also contribute to the popularity of destination icons, especially in the age of social networks, by posting photos of their travels. All this encourages the desire of the broader tourist population to visit such destination icons. Enormous growth in tourists taking photos of specific places and posting them on social networks helps to reinforce the impression of *something particularly valuable*. Thus, already in the second half of the 20th century, the internet was one of the levers for the transformation of the Adriatic lighthouses into tourist icons. Although at that time even tourists were not allowed to enter the lighthouses, tourists were happy to take photos with them in the background.

A destination icon, a symbol of a specific locality, destination and tourist country, is a particularly useful marketing feature to strengthen the tourist image and the impression of the diversity of the tourist country on the global market. Recent research has shown that destination icons are an important reason to visit and contribute to the attractiveness of a destination (Morrison, 2013). Destination icons are classified in the literature as typical attractive factors. In the development of specialised tourist offers, destination icons are the source of sustainable commercial ideas (Becken, 2005; Šerić, 2019b).

Destination icons are memorable subjective symbols in the minds of tourists. The emerging forms can be natural or built attractions, which the tourist recognises by their specific characteristics and whose peculiarity tempts him to take at least one photo of them. From these facts arises the need for planning and management of destination icons.

Destination icons with cultural and historical features are particularly popular among tourists today (Prorok et al., 2019). Historical facts, stories and legends associated with such destination icons provide extensive opportunities for the design and development of special tourism content. Destination icons also help differentiate local tourism offerings (Pearce et al., 2003). Complex competitive relationships in the global tourism supply market make it necessary to identify new potential content from which recognisable destination icons can be created. Cultural and historical heritage is one such resource (Becken, 2005). Tourists recognise the monumental heritage even without additional marketing promotion. It was the same with lighthouses, decades before the idea of commercialising them for tourism (Jakšić Stojanović & Šerić, 2018). Lighthouses attracted the attention of the first tourists visiting the Adriatic region, so some of them were recorded as motifs on old postcards. After the launch of the Stone Lights project, the public's interest in this cultural and historical heritage grew, so that reports in magazines were published more and more frequently.

After the first season of tourist stays in the lighthouses, advertising also spreads through social networks. The possibility of spreading advertising through the internet and social networks is a form of promotion that should definitely be practised for the category of specialised tourism products (Chaffey et al., 2003; Šerić & Jerkić, 2014; Sheth et al., 2001). The growing public interest in lighthouses and lighthouse heritage led to the increasing selection of lighthouse motifs for stamps.

All this has further strengthened the perception of lighthouses on the Adriatic as recognisable icons of tourist destinations (Jakšić Stojanović & Šerić, 2018).

Photos of individual lighthouses were used as a reminder of the umbrella brand within the *Stone Lights* project. In the second phase of the project implementation, a photo exhibition *Croatian Lighthouses (Hrvatski svjetionici)* was set up with a display that is exhibited in most capitals around the world. The result of the long-term collection of testimonies, stories and legends related to Adriatic lighthouses are the published books *Stone Lights – Stories and Legends about Adriatic Lighthouses, about the places where they were built and about their seabed (Kamena Svjetla – priče i legende o jadranskim svjetionicima, o mjestima na kojima su izgrađeni i o njihovom podmorju)* in the Republic of Croatia (Šerić, 2004) and *The Montenegrin Lighthouses as Destination Icons in Montenegro* (Jakšić Stojanović & Šerić, 2018). The cross-border university cooperation of the author with a colleague from the University of Podgorica, Montenegro – Anđela Jakšić Stojanović – resulted in the project of tourism valorisation of lighthouses in Montenegro, the details of which are published in the book *Montenegrin Lighthouses as Destination Icons* (Jakšić Stojanović & Šerić, 2018).

10.3. Developing an Idea for the Commercialisation of a New Specialised Tourism Product: *Summer Holidays at the Lighthouse*

The lighthouses on the eastern Adriatic were built more than 200 years ago. Decades after their construction, the possibility was not considered, mainly because of the complexity of the transfer, which depends on the hydrometeorological conditions at sea. Transportation by slow working boats and the isolation of the lighthouse were also the reason lighthouse keepers lived there with their families, grew vegetables in landscaped gardens, kept poultry, and sometimes goats and sheep.

Sailors perceived lighthouses as attractive destination icons (Šerić, 2011; Šerić & Perišić, 2012; Šerić, Peronja, et al., 2020). When sailing in the surrounding waters, they expressed interest in visiting them, taking photos under them, etc. In the past, lighthouses were objects with a special access regime, so few sailors took photos near the fenced yards of the lighthouse. With the development of the internet, the number of photos of Adriatic lighthouses increased. The development of digital photo equipment and the emergence of social networks have made photos of lighthouses even more widespread on the internet. The modern association of the lighthouse (as an attractive, mystical historical building in an ecologically preserved environment with a preserved underwater biodiversity) has replaced the earlier impression of a building with a ban on access to the unemployed in a remote, coastal, isolated destination, increasingly encouraged the desires of other tourist segments besides boaters to stay there (Šerić, 2004, 2008, 2011).

The tourist valorisation of lighthouses began in the late 90s of the 20th century after the automation of their lights. Since most of the lighthouses were built on remote islands, the lighthouse keepers and their families stayed there constantly, as they were busy every day maintaining the equipment and switching the lights on and off. The automation of the beacons and the introduction of remote monitoring allowed the lighthouse keepers to stay at the lighthouses that were strategically important for the safety of navigation (the most remote islands). The construction of fast working boats by Company Y, the company that manages the lighthouses on behalf of the Republic of Croatia, made it possible to employ lighthouse keepers in shifts (for 15 or 30 days). The lighthouse keepers no longer had to live there permanently with their families (before the automation of the lighthouses and the remote monitoring of their work, four families lived in the lighthouse at a time). The development of the idea of lighthouse tourism was stimulated by the free accommodation capacity of the lighthouse buildings and with the aim of additional income to help finance the salaries of the lighthouse keepers at as many lighthouses as possible. Despite the automation of the beacons and remote monitoring of their operation, the buildings tend to deteriorate without keepers. In addition, lighthouse keepers can fulfil their role in the national navigation safety system that enables environmental monitoring, regular report-ing and notification by radio, assistance to victims of marine accidents in surrounding waters, daily monitoring of hydrometeorological equipment installed on numerous lighthouses and regular reporting of measurements to the National Hydrometeorological Institute.

In the last decade of the 20th century, tourist interest in isolated offshore destinations, ecological oases with an intact landscape and underwater world, increased (Barros et al., 2011; Botti et al., 2009; Buhalis & Foerste, 2015; Buhalis et al., 2019; Dukić et al., 2011; Jafari & Xiao, 2021; Jakšić Stojanović et al., 2019b; Meler & Ham, 2012; Meler & Magaš, 2014; Ringer, 2013; Ruhanen et al., 2019). The development of the idea of tourism commercialisation of lighthouses was also stimulated by the declaration of lighthouse buildings as cultural and historical heritage. Such a feature of a location or building also contributes to increasing tourist interest in visiting and staying there (Aas et al., 2005; Cuccia et al., 2013; UN, Ending Poverty, https://www.un.org/en/sections/i, 2020).

10.4. Company Y Split: A State-Owned Company That Manages Navigation Safety on Behalf of the Republic of Croatia

The Republic of Croatia, a maritime country located on the eastern coast of the Adriatic Sea, is reminiscent of European Polynesia with its more than 1,000 islands, islets and rocks on a water area of about 30,000 km². Although the Croatian part of the Adriatic coast is about 1,000 km long, the total length of the coastal belt together with the islands is six times longer. The exceptional indentation and natural beauty of the Croatian part of the Adriatic Sea attract numerous sailors, so that today the largest part of the European charter fleet is moored in the marinas of the eastern Adriatic. If we take into account the density of other maritime traffic (merchant ships sailing from Otranto to the major ports of the northern Adriatic in Croatia, Slovenia and Italy), the importance of the proper functioning of more than 1,000 maritime signalling facilities under the responsibility of the company Y, whose core activity is the construction and maintenance of maritime signalling facilities and maritime radio service related to the danger and safety of navigation, becomes clear. Due to its importance for the safety of navigation, the operation of Company Y is directly subject to the supervision of the Croatian government. The operation of Company Y represents the continuity of the lighthouse service since the Austro-Hungarian Monarchy in the 19th century, when most of the approximately 50 lighthouses were built (the first was built in 1810), of which 48 are still in operation today. Despite the complete automation and remote monitoring of the beacons, lighthouse crews continue to operate in 16 of the most important lighthouses, evenly distributed every 30 nautical miles of the waterway along the eastern Adriatic coast, 330 nautical miles from Saint Andrew/ Sveti Andrija lighthouse of Dubrovnik to the Savudrija lighthouse on the western cape of the Istrian peninsula. Of particular importance are the Palagruža lighthouse, the most prominent lighthouse 74 nautical miles from the coast, located on a volcanic archipelago between the Italian and Croatian coasts, and the Porer lighthouse, which marks the busy waterway around the north-western cape of the Istrian peninsula and the approach to the port of Pula.

Today, about 40 lighthouse keepers work in shifts to ensure proper operation of navigation equipment and facilities, maintenance of lighthouse buildings, collection of meteorological data, monitoring of marine pollution, timely fire warnings and much more. Despite Company Y's constant efforts to preserve abandoned lighthouse buildings of exceptional historical and cultural value from decay due to automation, the limiting factor is the permanent lack of funding for their preservation, and many buildings are in poor condition due to extreme environmental conditions.

The idea of converting attractive lighthouse buildings for commercial tourism was realised in 1999 with the *Stone Lights* project, which to date has renovated more than 20 lighthouse buildings, where tourist apartments (3–4 star category) aıe 90% occupied during the summer season, and those with a power supply are occupied for 6 months or more.

The goal of the *Stone Lights* project is to use tourism revenues from the commercialisation of the lighthouse to self-finance the maintenance of existing and the creation of new tourist apartments and buildings at other lighthouses that are classified as attractive tourist destinations. In addition to 48 lighthouses, Company Y also maintains more than 1,000 other maritime signalling facilities. Company Y performs regular maintenance and emergency operations after the lights go out by coordinating seven navigation areas, located in all major Croatian ports. In addition to small boats for the needs of the lighthouse keepers, each navigation area also has a modern speedboat, which, thanks to its speed of about 23 knots and its exceptional maritime characteristics, can reach even the most distant lighthouse comfortably. In addition to supplying the lighthouse keeper and maintaining the maritime signalling facilities, the boats are also used for the urgent needs of the local population in special situations and represent a potential for organising tourist trips to the lighthouse.

10.5. Commercialisation and Market Positioning

Tourist commercialisation of lighthouse buildings, where the ownership of the land on which they were built was in some cases not regulated in the land registers, presented a complex challenge in the legal sense. Based on the approval of the Croatian government for the tourism valorisation of the lighthouse, the necessary legal steps were taken. In order to be able to legally regulate the financial investments in the renovation and reconstruction of lighthouse buildings, where the ownership of the land on which they were built was transferred from the local self-government units to the Republic of Croatia (Company Y is a state-owned company), business agreements on public partnerships were also approved. On this basis, the contracts were concluded for the multi-year lease, refurbishment and tourism valorisation of part of the lighthouse buildings that are not commercialised for tourism by Company Y. Lease concessions with private investors interested in lighthouse buildings, the lease of which is stipulated through a public tender, are concluded for a period of 5 or 10 years with the possibility of extending the cooperation. A concessionaire carrying out a tourist activity on a lighthouse maintains the lighthouse building in its entirety, while Company Y is responsible for the maintenance of technical equipment and operation of lights in the lighthouse and other equipment connected with the navigation safety system (automatic switching on and off and remote monitoring).

10.6. Management of the *Stone Lights* Tourism Project and Brand

Since the beginning of the commercialisation of the *Stone Lights* project, the tourism revenues generated are used for the ongoing maintenance of the lighthouse buildings for tourist accommodation and the rehabilitation of other lighthouse buildings without lighthouse keepers (Šerić, 2008). The project assumes the implementation of sustainable and responsible tourism standards. Electricity from renewable sources is used (solar panels with batteries and wind generators). Solar water heaters have been installed. The maximum daily consumption of hygienic water (150 litres/person) was set according to the purification capacity of the hygienic wastewater of each lighthouse (absorbents and bio-pits). Autochthonous plants in the vicinity of the lighthouse are watered with recycled sanitary wastewater (Šerić et al., 2002). Daily water consumption is controlled by programmed filling of daily sanitary water containers (depending on the number of guests in the apartment). When the available amount of water is used up, there is no more water in the apartment for the rest of the day. Guests will be advised of the maximum daily hygienic water consumption allowed when booking accommodation. The maximum accommodation capacity of each lighthouse intended for tourist accommodation is also based on the capacity of daily treatment of hygienic wastewater through absorption and bio-pits. There are also rules for waste disposal that guests must follow. Frequent warnings may be followed by termination of stay in the lighthouse without refund and registration of guests in the so-called *black book*, which gives the service provider the right to refuse future booking of a guest who has violated the rules of conduct in the lighthouse (Šerić & Luković, 2010). In 2000, the collection, sorting and recycling of waste was regulated similarly to the standards that the European Union would adopt 10 years later. Therefore, at the time of commercialisation, the *Stone Lights* project was ahead of its time. Inorganic waste, including construction debris, is collected and brought ashore for disposal. Organic waste is used for planting around the lighthouse. The rules of conduct have also been established for plants and animals, underwater flora and fauna and archaeological sites if they are located near the lighthouse.

Marketing project management is primarily based on publicity. The focus on publicity is due to the core business of Company Y (navigation safety) – the company that manages the lighthouses. The cost of economic propaganda for the secondary activity would be controversial in accounting. Advertising is effective for lighthouse tourism and due to the perception of tourists – mystical old buildings in remote and inaccessible places. This stimulates the imagination of tourists, who like to share their assumptions and impressions on social networks after their stay. Their impressions are also interesting for media and journalists who want to have such an experience. Media abroad have published dozens of articles and reports about tourist accommodation in Adriatic lighthouses. Along the way, they also write about the history of the lighthouse tradition, historical events, stories and legends related to the individual locations of the lighthouses. To date, several television programs about lighthouses have been recorded and broadcast on the national TV programs of France, Switzerland, Italy, Sweden, Belgium and other countries (Šerić, Jakšić Stojanović, et al., 2023).

Over the past 20 years of the commercialisation of the *Stone Lights* project, the eponymous brand became an association for a unique experience of a special experience of the former life of lighthouse keepers and their families on isolated offshore islands. Some of the sales intermediaries (travel agencies) have successfully used the *Stone Lights* brand as a catalyst for strengthening the visibility of their own offer and for co-branding purposes (*adriatica.net, Columbus, Adriatic.hr, Atlas Air tours, Maestral,* etc.).

The worldwide media presence of the project and the *Stone Lights* brand led to a new category – *lighthouse tourism* – which was also scientifically presented in the *Encyclopedia of Tourism Management and marketing* (Buhalis, 2022). Tour operators also used lighthouses as a motif on the covers of their annual catalogues. Catalogues printed in the tens of thousands also helped strengthen the *Stone Lights* brand.

Publicity of the *Stone Lights* project and brand contributed to the international visibility of the Company Y. The relationship between the *Stone Lights* and *Company Y* brands is also interesting. *Company Y's* core business – navigation safety as part of its corporate identity – was transferred to the *Stone Lights* brand. Thus, transfers to even distant lighthouses are not perceived as a kind of risk but as a unique tourist experience, about which tourists also like happy to share their impressions via social networks. The *Stone Lights* brand identity was intensively used in the marketing management of the project. This is reflected in the historical associations and traditions of the lighthouse service in the Adriatic, the safety of navigation and innovations in maritime signalling, as well as the adventurous challenge of this specialised tourist offer. The personality of the brand was communicated in accordance with the standards of responsible and sustainable tourism – many existing (energy from renewable sources) and some original ecological technological solutions by Company Y experts were implemented. Thanks to the implementation of numerous ecological solutions, which have also become part of the identity of the Stone Lights brand, Company Y was awarded an *Eco Oscar* of the Ministry of Nature and Environment in the category of Tourism and Environment. This recognition has also been used in project and brand marketing management activities.

Thanks to all this, a tourist stay in the lighthouses of the Adriatic is recognised as a unique experience of Robinson tourism, without renouncing the benefits of civilisation. Only the rules of responsible and sustainable tourism apply, meeting the highest ecological standards. Safe transfer to the most remote offshore islands, adequate supply of drinking and sanitary water, electricity from renewable sources, isolated stay in a protected landscape and accommodation in a facility that is part of the protected cultural and historical heritage ensured the differentiation of the specialised tourism product lighthouse tourism and the personality of the brand *Stone Lights*. The project manager worked in brand management from the launch until 2008 and his departure from the company:

- Continuously reminding the global tourism market of the offer by emphasising the *Stone Lights* brand and *spreading the story* about the brand in articles and reports in written and audio-visual media in the country and abroad.
- Maintaining the brand's market position and strengthening its image by gradually introducing new tourist accommodation lighthouses to the market.

- Promoting public–private partnership agreements with entities that have adopted lighthouses in the concession for tourism valorisation, where the ownership of the land on which they are built has not yet been settled.
- Introduction of new contents during the weekly tourist stay of the guest in the lighthouse (organised fishing with the lighthouse keepers, joint preparation of the catch in the local way, contests for the most impressive photos of the lighthouse, etc.).

The *Stone Lights* brand is positioned as a tourist stay in an unusual environment with pleasant microclimatic conditions. The image created by the sustainable and responsible tourism valorisation of a valuable cultural and historical heritage in a sensitive natural landscape is a confirmation of the implemented high civilisational standards. The complex content of the brand of this specialised offer contributes to the recognisability of the national identity of the Republic of Croatia, a recognisable maritime tourist Mediterranean country. The *Stone Lights* brand is an example of the practical valorisation of a valuable national resource through an original, specialised tourism offer. Despite the accommodation far from civilisation, on a remote island in sometimes unstable hydrometeorological conditions, the identity of the entity that offers this accommodation (the company *Company Y* – safety of navigation) contributes to the impression of safety for tourists, as a result of which the structure of visitors is dominated by different age groups. Standardising the experience of managing this tourist brand, it is possible to think about the sustainable development of new specialised tourism products based on valuable national resources.

Today, more than 20 years after the launch of the *Stone Lights* project, the brand is unfortunately in the *graveyard* zone. After the transfer of Company Y's project manager to the Faculty of Economics in Split in 2008, all brand management activities and most brand and project promotion activities were discontinued. Company Y's core business of shipping safety limits management's ability to justify the cost of marketing activities.

The interest not only of Company Y but also of the Ministry of Tourism of the Republic of Croatia should be to bring the *Stone Lights* brand back to the centre of interest of the global tourism market. Especially because even today, after more than 20 years of tourist accommodation in lighthouses, such experiences are commented on social networks as unique experiences, reminiscent of the years of the first decade after commercialisation, when accommodation in some lighthouses had to be booked 2 years in advance during the peak tourist season. It is interesting to note that the prices of accommodation have not been significantly adjusted since 2005 and, at the old level, do not contribute to the impression of exclusivity of a tourist stay in the lighthouses on the Adriatic. Moreover, there are less than 150 beds in total. Despite all this, the *Stone Lights* brand still attracts tourists who come across this offer for the first time. Regardless, it needs to be positioned in a new market niche, which requires a marketing plan and a programme of activities for its repositioning, i.e. *rebranding*.

Today, any specialised tourist offer based on cultural and historical heritage is a potential tourist attraction (Šerić, 2011). If the tourist clientele perceives it as a real attraction, this is a prerequisite for premium prices for content related to it (adapted from Fleisher & Bensoussan, 2003). The focus of the national tourism offer on specific cultural and historical heritage content contributes to year-round tourist visits (Šerić & Talijančić, 2011). Microclimatic conditions are no longer of primary importance when planning a trip to such a receptive country (Šerić, 2017).

Global tourism demand shows a particular interest in authentic cultural and historical heritage, as well as national heritage (Buhalis & Sinarta, 2019). Apart from the profitability of the tourist offer based on these contents, they also contribute to the recognition of national identity. Countries with centuries-old historical traditions attract the attention of today's tourists (Prorok et al., 2019). Based on these facts, it is recommended that a receptive country with a rich cultural and historical heritage should base its management concept for the national tourist offer precisely on these contents. The standards of responsible and long-term sustainable tourism valorisation should be observed.

The presented specialised tourism product *Stone Lights* is a practical example of the sustainable commercialisation of the valuable cultural and historical heritage. The implementation of responsible and sustainable tourism standards contributes not only to the preservation of the commercialised cultural and historical heritage but also to the increase of its value through continuous investment, maintenance and rehabilitation works. This is in accordance with the fundamental goal of the project – to restore the entire lighthouse heritage in the waters of the Republic of Croatia and to create a model for its continuous maintenance based on the funds received from tourism commercialisation. The surplus of the generated profit can be used for the salaries of the lighthouse keepers, which at the same time would allow the employees, who are primarily concerned with the safety of navigation, to be more involved in the area of tourist services at the lighthouses. In the future, this could also be the way to reintroduce human crews at all lighthouses, despite automation. The prerequisite is that in addition to the tourist apartments, the lighthouse buildings also have at least one studio apartment for the accommodation of the lighthouse keeper.

The *Stone Lights* project also served to promote the lighthouses of the Adriatic and the lighthouse heritage. The project transformed lighthouses into specific destination icons on the global tourism market (Jakšić Stojanović & Šerić, 2018). In the following years, the model was used in the region to create other categories of destination icons (Jakšić Stojanović et al., 2020). Accompanying marketing activities can also be used to promote other specialised tourism products based on cultural and historical content (international photo exhibition *Croatian Lighthouses* – set up in selected galleries in many capitals around the world). Reports in high-circulation daily newspapers also contributed to the global visibility of this special tourism product: *Le Figaro*, France (circulation of more than 330,000 copies), *Gazeta Wyborcza*, Poland (circulation of more than 540,000 copies), *Saarbrucker Zeitung*, Germany (circulation of more than 180,000 copies), as well as an article about the *Stone Lights* project published on the front page of the Yahoo portal in 2005.

With the resignation of Company Y's project manager, these modest brand management activities also ceased. Today, the project is in a phase of stagnation, so the concept of rejuvenation of the *Stone Lights* brand is being considered. It is necessary to bring it out of *the graveyard* zone through repositioning. The existing market position of the brand restricts the price calculation. Tourist traffic at lighthouses is decreasing, as is the value perception of tourist stays at lighthouses (Šerić, Peronja, et al., 2020). Given the worldwide popularity of the *Stone Lights* brand, this specialised tourist offer can be effectively repositioned. Branding activities need to be resumed, building on best practices (photo exhibitions Croatian Lighthouses and *More than light and salt: 200 years of Croatian lighthouses (Više od svjetla i soli: 200 godina Hrvatskih svjetionika)*. There are also new opportunities for cross-border tourism and scientific cooperation by connecting national projects for tourism valorisation of lighthouses in the Republic of Croatia and Montenegro. With the project *The Art of the Lighthouses* in Montenegro and the publication of the scientific monograph *The Montenegrin Lighthouses as Destination Icons* (Jakšić Stojanović & Šerić, 2018), it is possible to encourage the Ministry of the Republic of Croatia to support the revival of the *Stone Lights* brand. Tourist commercialisation of Adriatic lighthouses should remain under state supervision (Company Y is a state-owned company), as this segment of cultural and historical heritage represents an invaluable asset. Planned and continuous activities for branding a specialised tourism product are a prerequisite for maintaining the competitiveness, visibility and attractiveness of the specific offer. Such projects are a useful marketing lever for strengthening the tourist image and national identity of the host country.

Unfortunately, the story of lighthouse tourism in the Republic of Croatia is currently stopped due to unclear and illogical legal regulations related to economic activities on the maritime property. This threatens the renewed construction destruction of the lighthouse buildings, today protected cultural monuments. The new Law on Maritime Property in the Republic of Croatia enables the arbitrary imposition of additional tax for *economic activities deemed to be carried out on maritime property*. The Customs Administration of the Republic of Croatia is authorised to implement this regulation, i.e. the collection of the new tax levy, pursuant to the *Law on Concessions*. The interpretation of the Customs Administration (the institution responsible for the implementation of the *Law on Concessions*) is that *lighthouses serve to regulate maritime traffic, so they are considered part of maritime property*. It is a paradox that not a single lighthouse building on the coast of the Republic of Croatia is located in an area that is considered a maritime property. As a result of such an interpretation, during the year of 2022, Company Y and all small concessionaires of lighthouse buildings were retroactively charged an additional tax levy (towards the new *Law on Concessions* in the Republic of Croatia is in force since 2018). In addition to the cumulative tax burden (in addition to the existing tax for tourist services and tax to profit), it imposes an illogical increase in accommodation prices, which would make this offer uncompetitive in relation to potential replacement specialised tourist products that can be considered under the category of *Robinson tourism*.

With this scenario, the Croatian Parliament, by accepting the new *Law on Maritime Property*, took the first step towards extinguishing lighthouse tourism, a specialised original tourist product that even has meanwhile become part of the national identity.

Lighthouse tourism as developed and commercialised in the Republic of Croatia was recognised in the academic world by the inclusion of a special chapter by authors Šerić and Jakšić Stojanović in the world's first scientific encyclopedia – *Management and Marketing in Tourism* (2022), edited by Professor Dimitrios Buhalis.

But there is also a wider context because Adriatic lighthouses are not only Croatian, but also European cultural and historical heritage, given that they were built by the Austro-Hungarian Monarchy. With the subsequent borders demarcation, they belonged to Yugoslavia, and finally to the Republic of Croatia, where Company Y, a state company in accordance with the *Law on Company Y*, manages them on behalf of the Republic of Croatia. Based on the decisions and approvals of previous Governments of the Republic of Croatia, the project of tourism valorisation of the lighthouse was realised. Sustainable tourism commercialisation of Adriatic lighthouses provided the funds needed for the renovation of all lighthouse buildings. Departmental Ministries in the Republic of Croatia did not provide funds for this purpose in their budgets, and since the 90s of the 20th century, after the automation of the lights in the lighthouse towers, Company Y no longer has the obligation to maintain the lighthouse buildings. With the automation of the lights in the lighthouse towers, the lighthouse buildings lost their original purpose (residential buildings for the families of lighthouse keepers). The tourism commercialisation of vacant parts of the lighthouse buildings provided not only funds for ongoing investment maintenance of the buildings but also enabled the return of the lighthouse keepers, who today stay there in monthly shifts, without their families. Thus, lighthouse tourism contributed to a higher level of navigation safety because man is still the most important link in this system.

The publication of this scientific book is a small step in encouraging new thinking in the parliaments of the Republic of Croatia and the European Union to bring the national regulations of the *Law on Maritime* Property in line with European standards and maintain lighthouse tourism so that not happens the fate of these cultural and historical buildings in some Mediterranean countries.

Lighthouse tourism in the Adriatic and the brand *Stone Lights* are a model of sustainable preservation of the lighthouse heritage, which became globally recognised with the setting of the Croatian lighthouses international photo exhibition. To date, that exhibition has been staged in more than 200 world capitals.

Lighthouse tourism is based on the highest ecological standards – restrictions on the number of tourists who can stay at the lighthouse at the same time, collection and recovery of all types of waste, energy from renewable sources, recovery of sanitary waste water and its use for the maintenance of horticultural plantations. Lighthouse tourism is a recognisable category in green tourism. The ecological solutions implemented in the *Stone Lights* project at the beginning, in the year of 2001, resulted by the national Eco Oscar in the *Tourism and Environment category*. Many articles have been published about tourism experiences during the unforgettable stay at the lighthouses (in *National Geographic*, *Le Figaro*, *Playboy* and others). Through the touristic valorisation of the lighthouse heritage, a valuable component of the European cultural and historical heritage, many lighthouses have been restored and presented to the world. However, threats of new national legal regulations due to the possibility of additional tax of lighthouse tourism may result in the suspension of this specialised tourist offer. Due to the lack of funds, the roofs of the lighthouse buildings will collapse, the windows and doors will probably be bricked up, but despite everything, the buildings will eventually become ruins. Perhaps the publication of this scientific book will stimulate the thinking of national political elites in the Republic of Croatia to adjust regulations with European standards and thus stop the disappearance of an important national feature of maritime identity – the lighthouse heritage. The carelessness of the national authorities on part of the European cultural and historical heritage of the Republic of Croatia can generate negative publicity even.

Regardless of the final destiny, the story of the Adriatic lighthouses was permanently recorded in the motion picture (starring Franco Nero) by Jakov Sedlar 'Houses of light, the story of Croatian lighthouses'. The film shot at the locations of the Adriatic lighthouses during its premier screenings in 2022 was awarded several international awards in the category of cultural heritage promotion in tourism.

Chapter 11

Final Conclusions

Today, the continuity of the development of specialised tourism products is a prerequisite for maintaining the attractiveness and competitiveness of any national tourism offer. The increase in tourism migration at the global level is a prerequisite for the growth of the share of tourism revenues in the gross national product of countries where tourism is not a strategic sector of the economy. The number of receptive countries that recognise the tourism industry as a strategic commitment is increasing. The competitive relationships of the receptive tourism countries are becoming more complex. The spending of tourists who do not board is also increasing. Considering all these facts, the importance of specialised tourism content is also increasing. The still modest scientific research and the lack of scientific literature dealing with the design, development and management of specialised tourist content were the impetus for the preparation and publication of this work. Experiences from the author's practice served as arguments for the presented guide. This has resulted in an unusual work that will be used for the training of tourism professionals involved in the design and marketing of new specialised tourism content, as well as for the training of tourism students.

The supply of specialised tourism content on a global scale is growing. However, much of this content has been developed unsystematically. The consequence of such a development is the frequent scepticism of tourists towards much specialised content. Various fears (that the experience will not match the advertised level, that the content will be disproportionately expensive, etc.) lead to a slower decision to make a test purchase. Tourists also perceive certain specialised tourism facilities as experiments, offers designed to test the market, etc. Such perception also does not contribute to a faster decision to make a test purchase. After the commercialisation of specialised tourist contents, they are often left to the market instead of systematically managing their offer, marketing them and managing their brands.

The originality of a specialised tourism product is not a prerequisite for its attractiveness and the intuitive decision of tourists to make a test purchase. Appropriate positioning in a specific market niche may additionally attract the attention of the tourist audience, but a quicker decision to make a test purchase will only be made by a narrower segment whose needs, desires and value

Specialised Tourism Products, 139–142
Copyright © 2024 Neven Šerić, Ivana Kursan Milaković and Ivan Peronja
Published under exclusive licence by Emerald Publishing Limited
doi:10.1108/978-1-83549-408-020241011

standards the specific content best meets. The proportion of tourists attracted to the new specialised tourism content for the first time in the destination where it is offered will also be modest. This fact discourages those working in tourism, and especially potential investors, to invest in the development of more complex specialised products. On the other hand, the desire to maintain the competitiveness of the destination encourages the introduction of new content in the tourist offer. The result is modest budgets spent on such content and its unsystematic development. If such content attracts the additional attention of some tourists who visit the destination for the first time, the question arises whether they will return the next season. Systematic development and management of a specialised tourism product requires strict adherence to high marketing standards, from idea generation to communication with tourists, in order to encourage their loyalty to such content and the destination where it is offered.

The return on investment in the development of specialised tourism content, i.e. the share of its sales in the total tourism revenues of the receiving country, depends on many factors. In addition to content differentiation, the way in which a specific new offer is presented and promoted to target markets is also important. Is it in line with current tourism trends? How specific is the new specialised content in synergy with the existing offerings of the destination in which it is being offered? Has the development process been rationalised from idea to launch in the tourism market? Has the potential demand for new content in the target markets of broadcast tourism been correctly assessed? Based on the answers to the above questions, it is possible to simulate the sales intensity of new specialised content after its introduction to the market. However, the sales potential of these contents in the following years remains a mystery. To solve this puzzle, it is necessary to evaluate the availability of concrete resources on which the new specialised tourism product is based. What is the allowable intensity of consumption of these resources? Are the standards for long-term and sustainable utilisation of these resources defined at the local level? Today, climate change must also be taken into account. The seasonality of tourist visitation in the destination where the new specialised tourism product is to be offered can also significantly affect the growth of its sales. In the presented approach to the development of a new specialised tourism product, many of the mentioned constraints are analysed in terms of opportunities. It is a fact that systematically developed specialised tourist facilities help to reduce the seasonality of tourist visits.

The perception of tourists about the offer of a receptive tourist country is slowly changing. By developing new specialised tourism content, it is possible to significantly influence this perception.

Certain specialised tourism facilities, while the focus of interest for a narrower tourism segment, are attracting the attention of a broader tourism audience. Tourists who decide to make a test purchase of a specialised tourism product often become advertisers for such content. This is also confirmed by photo series on social networks. Tourists willingly pay premium prices for specialised tourism products that are impressive in terms of content. Destinations that offer such services reduce the problem of seasonality. Another incentive to purchase a new sample specialised tourism product is the impression of added value. The added value is to a significant extent a consequence of the impressions of the overall content. Therefore, systematically developed new specialised tourism products have a good chance of market success. The perception of the added value of a specialised tourism product is a consequence of the effective implementation of marketing and marketing tools during the development process. The potential of the contribution of specialised content to tourism development is also a lever for the social development of the country. The potential of this leverage is even greater for small post-transition countries. The increase in the number of tourism facilities is a prerequisite for new jobs and raising the standard of living of the local population. For this reason, the local population of the destination is often positive about the development of new specialised tourism products. New content is often the result of local initiatives.

Building the national tourist offer on a variety of specialised tourism products contributes to the differentiation of the recipient country. The growing number of such offers is also encouraged by the introduction of standards for responsible and sustainable tourism. The resources on which they are based mostly belong to the category of non-renewable resources, so it is necessary to introduce measures to monitor and control their consumption.

Even though specialised tourism products are desirable and necessary, they pose numerous risks for the stakeholders who invest money in their development. In addition to the aforementioned security risks, traffic, hydrometeorological and other risks also affect revenues from this content. The overall risks to investors in developing new tourism facilities are lower for facilities that can be offered year-round. Creative and attractive specialised tourism content with clear added value for tourists requires knowledge and experience, knowledge of tourist destination segments, as well as local traditions and culture. This is only part of the requirements to eventually offer an attractive autochthonous specialised tourism product. Care should also be taken in selecting the staff that will sell and participate in providing such content. Indigenous specialised tourism content also includes indigenous service personnel. Thus, indigenous tourism staff intrude as a desirable solution for this offering. These tourism personnel often lack expertise, so they are also part of the target audience of this book.

Continued development of new specialised tourism products will help extend the tourism season and reduce the seasonality of the local tourism economy. Best global practice and the experience presented in this book suggest that it is justified to balance tourism absorption capacities at national and local levels according to the geographical intensity of such an offer. Host tourism countries with large hotel establishments will have a difficult time adapting to this strategic alignment of tourism supply. Due to the structure and concentration of host capacity in these countries, the standards for responsible and sustainable utilisation of non-renewable resources are also lower. The higher intensity of consumption of these resources leads to a narrower range of specialised tourism products. The result is the prevailing seasonality of the tourism industry, mass tourism and everything related to it. In such an active environment, specialised tourist facilities have no perspective.

A long-term systematic approach is needed in tourism, both in the management of resources and in the management of tourist development, but also of tourism products. An uncontrolled increase in tourist visits, especially seasonal, leads to uncontrolled commercialisation and destruction of resources. This permanently wastes the opportunities for the development of many categories of specialised tourist content. Due to all these facts, the issue of developing specialised tourism products is important for any receptive country where tourism is a strategic activity. In practice, this means strengthening parliamentary democracy and reducing all forms of corruption and favouritism in the selection and ranking of proposals for new tourism content. Future research could also explore the internal and external motivations for specialised tourism products, such as lighthouses, dark tourism and solo female/male travellers. Such future studies might also include the variations across demographic characteristics like age, gender and education.

References

Aaker, D. (2001). *Strategic market management* (6th ed.). John Wiley & Sons, Inc.

Aaker, D. (2002). *Building strong brands*. Simon & Schuster.

Aaker, D., Batra, R., & Meyers, J. G. (1992). *Advertising management*. Prentice Hall.

Aas, C., Ladkin, A., & Fletcher, J. (2005). Stakeholder collaboration and heritage management. *Annals of Tourism Research, 32*(1), 28–48.

Akbar, M. D. (2017). Risk as a motivation for adventure tourist. *Journal on Hospitality and Tourism, 15*(1), 48–61.

Ambler, T. (2000). *Marketing and the bottom line: The new metrics of corporate wealth*. Prentice Hall.

Andersen, A., Hiebele, R., Kelly, T. B., & Katteman, C. (1998). *Best practices: Building your business with customer-focused solutions*. Simon & Schuster.

Andersen, A., & Petersen, A. (1993). Procedure for ranking efficient units in data envelopment analysis. *Management Science, 39*(10), 1261–1264.

Anderson, K., & Kerr, C. (2002). *Customer relationship management*. McGraw-Hill.

Andreasen, A. L. (2001). *Ethics in social marketing*. Georgetown University Press.

Angelevska Najdeska, K., & Rakicevik, G. (2012). Planning of sustainable tourism development. *Procedia – Social and Behavioral Sciences, 44*, 210–220.

Armenski, T., Gomezelj, D. O., Djurdjev, B., Ćurčić, N., & Dragin, A. (2012). Tourism destination competitiveness – Between two flags. *Economic Research, 25*(2), 485–502.

Baars, H., Kemper, H. G., Lasi, H., & Siegel, M. (2008). Combining RFID technology and business intelligence for supply chain optimization – Scenarios for retail logistics. In *Proceedings of the 41st Hawaii International Conference on System Sciences 2008*. https://www.researchgate.net/publication/4315039_Combining_RFID_Technology_and_Business_Intelligence_for_Supply_Chain_Optimization_Scenarios_for_Retail_Logistics

Baggio, R. (2020). The science of complexity in the tourism domain: A perspective article. *Tourism Review, 75*(1), 16–19.

Baker, B. (2007). *Destination branding for small cities: The essentials for successful place branding*. Creative Leap Books.

Baker, M., & Riley, M. (1994). New perspectives on productivity in hotels: Some advances and new directions. *International Journal of Hospitality Management, 13*(4), 297–311.

Barros, C. P., & Alves, F. P. (2004). Productivity in tourism industry. *International Advances in Economic Research, 10*(3), 215–225.

Barros, C. P., Botti, L., Peypoch, N., Robinot, E., Solonandrasana, B., & Assaf, A. G. (2011). Performance of French destinations: Tourism attraction perspectives. *Tourism Management, 32*(1), 141–146.

Barros, C. P., & Mascarenhas, M. J. (2005). Technical and allocative efficiency in a chain of small hotels. *Hospitality Management, 24*(3), 415–436.

Baruah, S. (2023). Risk of extreme tourism: The Titan submersible – A case study on high-risk adventures. https://www.cnbctv18.com/travel/rise-of-extreme-tourism-the-titan-submersible-a-case-study-on-high-risk-adventures-17083641.htm

Becken, S. (2005). The role of tourist icons for sustainable tourism. *Journal of Vacation Marketing*, *11*(1), 21–30.

Beeton, S. (2006). *Community development through tourism*. Landlinks Press.

Beresford Research. (2023). *Age range by generation*. https://www.beresfordresearch.com/age-range-by-generation/

Best, K. (2010). *The fundamentals of design management*. Ava Publishing SA.

Bi, G., Luo, Y., & Liang, L. (2011). Efficiency evaluation of tourism industry with data envelopment analysis (DEA): A case study in China. *Journal of China Tourism Research*, *7*(1), 104–116.

Bieger, T. (2000). *Management von Destinationen und Tourismusorganisationen*. Oldenbourg.

Bigne, J. E., Sancez, M. I., & Sanchez, J. (2001). Tourism image, evaluation variables and after-purchase behaviour: Inter-relationship. *Tourism Management*, *22*(6), 607–616.

Bilandžić, M. (2008). *Poslovno-obavještajno djelovanje: Business Intelligence u praksi*. AGM Zagreb.

Boes, K., Buhalis, D., & Inversini, A. (2016). Smart tourism destinations: Ecosystems for tourism destination competitiveness. *International Journal of Tourism Cities*, *2*(2), 108–124.

Bond, M. (2023). *Women travel statistics from women travel expert*. https://gutsytraveler.com/women-travel-statistics-women-travel-expert/

Borges, M., Hoppen, N., & Luce, F. B. (2009). Information technology impact on market orientation in e-business. *Journal of Business Research*, *62*, 883–890.

Borja de Mozota, B. (2003). *Design management: Using design to build brand value and corporate innovation*. DMI/Allworth Press.

Borovac Zekan, S., Rakušić, K., & Šerić, N. (2011). Using social networks in small business entrepreneurship. In *Proceedings of researching economic development and entrepreneurship in transition economies* (pp. 414–421). Faculty of Economics, University of Banja Luka.

Botti, L., Peypoch, N., Robinot, E., & Solonandrasana, B. (2009). Tourism destination competitiveness: The French regions case. *European Journal of Tourism Research*, *21*, 5–24.

Boyer, J., Frank, B., Green, B., Harris, T., & Van De Vanter, K. (2011). *Business intelligence strategy*. MC Press Online.

Brandt, C. (2023). *The impact of social media on the tourism industry*. https://givinggetaway.com/the-impact-of-social-media-on-the-tourism-industry

Brown, M. G. (2009). *Beyond the balanced scorecard: Improving business intelligence with analytics*. CRC Press.

Buckley, R. (2020). Rush as a key motivation in skilled adventure tourism: Resolving the risk recreation paradox. *Tourism Management*, *33*(4), 961–970.

Buhalis, D. (2000). Marketing the competitive destination of the future. *Tourism Management*, *2*(1), 97–116.

Buhalis, D. (2022). *Preface in encyclopedia of tourism management and marketing: Tourism management and marketing in transformation preface*. Edward Elgar Publishing. (Forthcoming).

Buhalis, D., & Foerste, M. (2015). SoCoMo marketing for travel and tourism: Empowering co-creation of value. *Journal of Destination Marketing & Management, 4*(3), 151–161.

Buhalis, D., Harwood, T., Bogičević, V., Viglia, G., Beldona, S., & Hofacker, C. (2019). Technological disruptions in service: Lessons from tourism and hospitality. *Journal of Service Management, 30,* 484–506.

Buhalis, D., & Law, R. (2008). Progress in information technology and tourism management: 20 years on and 10 years after the Internet—The state of eTourism research. *Tourism Management, 29*(4), 609–623.

Buhalis, D., & Park, S. (2021). *Journal of Product & Brand Management, 30*(1), 1–11.

Buhalis, D., & Sinarta, Y. (2019). Real-time co-creation and nowness service: Lessons from tourism and hospitality. *Journal of Travel & Tourism Marketing, 36*(5), 563–582.

Butler, R. W. (2020). Tourism carrying capacity research: A perspective article. *Tourism Review, 75*(1), 207–211.

Cantino, V., Culasso, F., & Racca, G. (2018). *Smart tourism.* McGraw Hill Education.

Cavalcanti, E. P. (2005). The relationship between business intelligence and business success. *Journal of Competitive Intelligence and Management, 3*(1), 3–11.

CBI, Ministry of Foreign Affairs. (2023). *The European market potential for nature tourism.* https://www.cbi.eu/market-information/tourism/nature-tourism/market-potential

Chaffey, D., Mayer, R., Johnston, K., & Ellis Chadwick, F. (2003). *Internet marketing – Strategy, implementation and practice.* Prentice Hall.

Cheng, M., & Edwards, D. (2015). Social media in tourism: A visual analytic approach. *Current Issues in Tourism, 18*(11), 1080–1087.

Churchill, I. (2002). *The market research.* South – Western.

Coasta, C. (2020). Tourism planning: A perspective paper. *Tourism Review, 75*(1), 198–202.

Condor. (2023). *Female travel. Statistics 2023.* https://www.condorferries.co.uk/female-travel-statistics

Cooper, C. (2021). *Essentials of tourism.* SAGE Publications Limited.

Cracolici, M. F., Nijkamp, P., & Rietveld, P. (2008). Assessment of tourism competitiveness by analyzing destination efficiency. *Tourism Economics, 14*(2), 325–342.

Crouch, I. G. (2007). *Modelling destination competitiveness – A survey and analysis of the impact of competitiveness attributes.* Cooperative Research Centre for Sustainable Tourism.

Cuccia, T., Guccio, C., & Rizzo, I. (2013). *Does UNESCO inscription affect the performance of tourism destinations? A regional perspective.* ACEI Working Papers Series, AWP-04-2013. https://doi.org/10.2139/ssrn.2225771

Cvetkoska, V., & Barišić, P. (2014). Measuring the efficiency of certain European countries in tourism: DEA window analysis. In *Book of Proceedings of the International May Conference on Strategic Management – IMKS14.* University of Belgrade.

Czinkota, M. R. (2000). *Marketing: Best practices.* The Dryden Press.

Dedcoğlu, B. B., Van Niekerk, M., Küçükergin, K. G., De Martino, M., & Okumuş, F. (2020). Effect of social media sharing on destination brand awareness and destination quality. *Journal of Vacation Marketing, 26*(1), 33–56.

Dibb, S., Simkin, L., Pride, M. W., & Ferrell, C. O. (2001). *Marketing concepts and strategies.* Houghton Mifflin.

Dolnicar, S. (2019). Market segmentation analysis in tourism: A perspective paper. *Tourism Review, 75*(1), 45–48.

Doyle, P. (2002). *Marketing management and strategy* (3rd ed.). Pearson Education Ltd.

Drucker, P. (1994). *Post capitalist society.* Harper & Row.

Dukić, B., Meler, M., & Katić, M. (2011). Relationship improvement model for visitors of the nature park Kopački rit through the usage of mobile technology. In *Proceedings of the 33rd International Conference on Information Technology Interfaces ITI 2011*, Cavtat, Croatia (pp. 385–390). IEEE.

Dwyer, L., Mellor, R., Livaic, Z., Edwards, D., & Kim, C. (2004). Attributes of destination competitiveness: A factor analysis. *Tourism Analysis, 9*(1), 91–101.

Edgell, D. L., Del Mastro, M. A., Smith, G., & Swanson, J. R. (2008). *Tourism policy and planning: Yesterday, today and tomorrow.* Elsevier, Butterworth Heinemann.

Evtushenko, A. V. (2013). The sensory marketing in the tourism business as the latest technology in the tourism product promotion. *International Relations. Economy. Local Lore. Tourism No 1086/2013*, 143–146.

Filipović, M. (2017). *Resursi za razvoj tamnog turizma na prostoru Dalmacije.* Ekonomski fakultet.

Fleisher, C. S., & Bensoussan, B. E. (2003). *Strategic and competitive analysis.* Prentice Hall.

Fletcher, A. (2003). *The art of looking sideways.* Phaidon London.

Foo, L. M., & Rosetto, A. (1998). *Cultural tourism in Australia – Characteristics and motivations: BTR Occasional Paper No. 27.* Bureau of Tourism Research.

Ghorbanzadeh, D., Zakieva, R. R., Kuznetsova, M., Ismael, A. M., & Ahmed, A. A. A. (2022). Generating destination brand awareness and image through the firm's social media. *Kybernetes, 52*(9), 3292–3314.

Giddy, J. K. (2018). Adventure tourism motivations: A push and pull factor approach. *Bulletin of Geography. Socio-Economic Series*, (42), 47–58.

Girish, P. (2020). Time for reset Covid-19 and tourism resilience. *Tourism Review International, 24*(2–3), 179–184.

GlobalData. (2023). *Social media in travel and tourism – Thematic intelligence.* https://www.globaldata.com/store/report/social-media-in-travel-and-tourism-theme-analysis/

Gossling, S., Scott, D., & Hall, C. M. (2020). Pandemic, tourism and global change: A rapid assessment of Covid-19. *Journal of Sustainable Tourism, 29*(1), 1–20.

Grbac, B., Dlačić, J., & First, I. (2008). *Trendovi marketinga.* Solutio Rijeka.

Gürer, B., & Kural, B. (2023). Push and pull motivations of sport climbers within the scope of outdoor and adventure tourism. *Journal of Quality Assurance in Hospitality & Tourism*, 1–20. https://doi.org/10.1080/1528008X.2023.2211787

Hadad, S., Hadad, Y., Malul, M., & Rosenboim, M. (2012). The economic efficiency of the tourism industry: A global comparison. *Tourism Economics, 18*(5), 931–940.

Hadianfar, N. (2021). Impact of social media marketing on consumer-based brand equity for tourism destination: Evidence from Isfahan, Iran. *International Journal of Digital Content Management, 2*(2), 149–170.

Hall, C. M., Scott, D., & Gossling, S. (2020). Pandemics, transformations and tourism: Be careful what you wish for. *Tourism Geographies, 22*(3), 577–598.

Hedin, H., Hirvensalo, I., & Vaarnas, M. (2011). *The handbook of market intelligence.* John Wiley & Sons.

Hitrec, H. (2012). *Hrvatske legende.* Školska knjiga.

Holm, M. R., Lugosi, P., Croes, R. R., & Torres, E. N. (2017). Risk-tourism, risk-taking and subjective well-being: A review and synthesis. *Tourism Management, 63*, 115–122.

Hooley, G. J., Saunders, J. A., & Piercy, N. F. (2004). *Marketing strategy and competitive positioning* (3rd ed.). Prentice Hall.

Hosany, S., Ekinci, Y., & Uysal, M. (2007). Destination image and destination personality. *International Journal of Culture, Tourism and Hospitality Research, 1*(1), 62–81.

Hosseini, S., Macias, R. C., & Garcia, F. A. (2022). The exploration of Iranian solo female travelers' experiences. *International Journal of Tourism Research, 24*(2), 256–269.

Idbenssi, S., Safaa, L., Perkumienė, D., & Škėma, M. (2023). Exploring the relationship between social media and tourist experiences: A bibliometric overview. *Social Sciences, 12*(8), 444.

Islam, M. T. (2021). Applications of social media in the tourism industry: A review. *SEISENSE Journal of Management, 4*(1), 59–68.

Jafari, J., & Xiao, H. (2021). *Encyclopedia of tourism.* Springer.

Jakšić Stojanović, A., Janković, M., & Šerić, N. (2019a). Montenegro as a high-quality health tourism destination: Trends and Perspectives. *African Journal of Hospitality, Tourism and Leisure, 8*(3), 1–9.

Jakšić Stojanović, A., Janković, M., & Šerić, N. (2019b). Montenegro as high-quality sports tourism destination – Trends and perspectives. *Sport Mont Journal (SMJ), 17*(1), 93–95.

Jakšić Stojanović, A., Janković, M., Šerić, N., & Vukilić, B. (2019). Branding of protected areas and National Parks: A case study of Montenegro. *African Journal of Hospitality, Tourism and Leisure, 8*(2), 1–9.

Jakšić Stojanović, A., & Šerić, N. (2018). *The Montenegrin lighthouses as destination icons.* University Mediterranean Podgorica Montenegro.

Jakšić Stojanović, A., & Šerić, N. (2019a). *Sports and health as corner stones of tourism development – Case study of Montenegro in sports science and human health – Different approaches.* Intech Open Limited. www.intechopen.com/about-intechopen

Jakšić Stojanović, A., & Šerić, N. (2019b). The art of the lighthouses – Montenegrin lighthouses as destination icons. In *IAI Academic Conference Proceedings: Education and Social Sciences Conference* (pp. 81–91). Cyril and Methodius University Skopje.

Jakšić Stojanović, A., Šerić, N., & Miljušković, M. (2020). *The Montenegrin bridges and their valorization.* Ministry of Science Government of Montenegro, University Mediterranean Podgorica Montenegro.

Jukšić Stojanović, A., Šerić, N., & Perišić, M. (2019). Marketing management of the lighthouse heritage in the function of strengthening the national identity on the global tourism market: Stone Lights (Croatia) and the art of the lighthouses (Montenegro). *Proceedings of the Faculty of Economics in East Sarajevo, 19*, 83–98.

Jenkins, B. (2020). Marginalizaciton within nerd culture: Racism and sexism within cosplay. https://www.researchgate.net/publication/341464848_Marginalization_within_Nerd_Culture_Racism_and_Sexism_within_Cosplay

Jerkić, I., & Šerić, N. (2014). Applicability of guerrilla marketing in e-business. In *E-Conference Proceedings 15th Paneuropean Shipping Conference*, Split.

Jobber, D. (2001). *Principles and practice of marketing* (3rd ed.). McGraw Hill.

Joly, D. (2010). *The dark tourist: Sightseeing in the world's unlikely holiday destinations.* Simon & Schuster.

Kancheva, I. K. (2017). *Going beyond 'Because it's there' – Multiple motivations for pursuing high-risk adventure activities.* PsyArXiv Preprints. https://osf.io/preprints/psyarxiv/pqdxc/

Kane, M. J., & Tucker, H. (2004). Adventure tourism: The freedom to play with reality. *Tourist Studies, 4*(3), 217–234.

Karaca, Ş., & Polat, G. (2022). The use of social media in cultural tourism. *Sivas Interdisipliner Turizm Araştırmaları Dergisi, 5*(1–2), 35–51.

Keller, L. K. (2003). *Strategic brand management.* Prentice Hall.

Kerin, A. R., & Peterson, A. R. (2004). *Strategic marketing problems.* Pearson Prentice Hall.

Kladou, S., & Kehagias, J. (2014). Developing a structural brand equity model for cultural destinations. *Journal of Place Management and Development, 7*(2), 112–125.

Koskinen, M., & Öhberg, L. (2014). *Profiling the adventure tourist: Case study New Zealand.* https://www.theseus.fi/bitstream/handle/10024/83741/Koskinen_Miia_Ohberg_Lotta.pdf?sequence=2

Kosmaczewska, J. (2014). Tourism interest and the efficiency of its utilization based on the example of the EU countries. *Oeconomia, 13*(1), 77–90.

Kotler, P., & Armstrong, G. (2001). *Principles of marketing* (9th ed.). Prentice Hall.

Kotler, P., Bowen, J., & Makens, J. (2010). *Marketing u ugostiteljstvu, hotelijerstvu i turizmu.* Mate d.o.o.

Kotler, P., Keller, K. L., Brady, M., Goodman, M., & Hansen, T. (2009). *Marketing management* (1st European ed.). Pearson/Prentice Hall.

Kozinets, R., de Valck, K., Wojnicki, A. C., & Wilner, S. J. S. (2010). Networked narratives: Understanding world-of-mouth marketing in online communities. *Journal of Marketing, 74*(March), 71–89.

Kumar, R. (2005). *Research methodology.* Sage Publications Ltd.

Kušen, E. (2002). Turizam i prostor klasifikacija turističkih atrakcija. *Prostor-znanstveni časopis za arhitekturu i urbanizam, 9*(1), 1–12.

Laws, E. (2002). *Tourism marketing: Quality and service management perspectives.* Continuum.

Lehman, D. R., & Winner, R. S. (2005). *Product management.* McGraw Hill.

Lidwell, W., Holden, K., & Butler, J. (2006). *Universal principles of design.* Mate.

Lockwood, T. (2009). *Design thinking: Integrating innovation, customer experience and brand value.* DMI Harvard Business Publishing.

Mansfeld, Y. (1992). From motivation to actual travel. *Annals of Tourism Research, 19*(3), 399–419.

Martín, J. C., Mendoza, C., & Román, C. A. (2015). A DEA travel-tourism competitiveness index. *Social Indicators Research*, 1–21.

Martin, P., & Priest, S. (1986). Understanding the adventure experience. *Journal of Adventure Education*, 3(1), 18–21.

McMillan Manley, K. (2016). What makes risk takers tempt fate? https://www.nationalgeographic.com/adventure/article/extreme-athletes-risk-taking

Meler, M. (2010). The necessity of using marketing metrics in tourism. In *Tourism & Hospitality Management 2010 Conference Proceedings*, Opatija, Hrvatska (pp. 138–152).

Meler, M., & Ham, M. (2012). Green marketing for green tourism. In *Tourism & Hospitality Management 2012 Conference Proceedings*, Opatija (pp. 130–139).

Meler, M., & Horvat, Đ. (2018). *Marketing Vina u Teoriji i Primjeni*. Edukator.

Meler, M., & Magaš, D. (2014). Sustainable marketing for sustainable development. In *Proceedings of 11th International Academic Conference*, Reykjavik (pp. 230–248).

Meler, M., & Škoro, M. (2013). (R)evolution of music marketing. In *Proceedings of 23rd CROMAR Congress: Marketing in a Dynamic Environment – Academic and Practical Insights*, Lovran, October 24–26, 2013 (pp. 52–65).

Meyers, S. L., Gamst, G., & Guarino, A. J. (2006). *Applied multivariate research*. Sage Publications Inc.

Mihić, M., & Šerić, N. (2007). Ethics and social responsibility as weakness or strength on the market in transition. In *Conference Proceedings 7th International Conference Enterprise in Transition 2007*. ISSN 1846-2618, UDK 339 (063).

Milano, C., Cheer, J. M., & Novelli, M. (2019). *Overtourism: Excesses, discontents and measures in travel and tourism*. Wallingford.

Mize. (2022). Positive and negative effects of social media on the tourism industry. https://www.hotelmize.com/blog/positive-and-negative-effects-of-social-media-on-the-tourism-industry

Modiano, D. (2011). *Adrenaline tourism: Chasing the thrill and the markets*. https://aboutourism.wordpress.com/2011/01/20/adrenaline-tourism-imagination-required

Morand, J. C., Cardoso, L., Pereira, A. M., Araújo-Vila, N., & de Almeida, G. G. F. (2021). Tourism ambassadors as special destination image inducers. *Enlightening Tourism. A Pathmaking Journal*, 11(1), 194–230.

Moro, S., & Rita, P. (2018). Brand strategies in social media in hospitality and tourism. *International Journal of Contemporary Hospitality Management*, 30(1), 343–364.

Morrison, A. M. (2013). *Marketing and managing tourism destinations*. Routledge.

Moss, L. T., & Atre, S. (2003). *Business intelligence roadmap*. Addison-Wesley.

Nasution, A. P., Pohan, M. Y. A., Ramadhan, D. A., Limbong, C. H., & Harahap, N. J. (2023). Factors affecting adventure tourist satisfaction: Evidence from Indonesia. *Innovative Marketing*, 19(2), 51–62.

Nath, K. (2023). Solo travel: A growing trend in 2023. https://www.traveldailymedia.com/solo-travel-a-growing-trend-in-2023/

Neumeier, M. (2009). *The designful company*. New Readers/Parsons Education.

Nikjoo, A., Markwell, K., Nikbin, M., & Hernández-Lara, A. B. (2021). The flag-bearers of change in a patriarchal Muslim society: Narratives of Iranian solo female travelers on Instagram. *Tourism Management Perspectives*, 38, 100817.

Nunkoo, R., Seetanah, B., & Agrawal, S. (2019). Innovation in sustainable tourism. *Tourism Review*, 74(2), 129–137.

Pearce, P., Morrison, A., & Moscardo, G. (2003). Individuals as tourist icons: A developmental and marketing analysis. *Journal of Travel Research, 10*(2003), 63–85.

Peter, J. P., & Donnelly, J. H. (2004). *Marketing management: Knowledge and skills* (7th ed.). Irwin.

Peypoch, N. (2007). On measuring tourism productivity. *Asia Pacific Journal of Tourism Research, 12*(3), 237–244.

Phillips, P., & Louvieris, P. (2005). Performance measurement systems in tourism, hospitality, and leisure small medium-sized enterprises: A balanced scorecard perspective. *Journal of Travel Research, 44*(2), 201–211.

Piercy, N. F. (2002). *Market-led strategic change: A guide to transforming the process of going to market* (3rd ed.). Butterworth-Heinemann.

Pike, S. (2008). *Destination marketing: An integrated marketing communication approach*. Elsevier.

Pineda, R. H., Svoboda, K. R., Wright, M. A., Taylor, A. D., Novak, A. E., Gamse, J. T., Eisen, J. S., & Ribera, A. B. (2004). Knockdown of Nav1. 6a Na+ channels affects zebrafish motoneuron development. https://zfin.org/ZDB-PUB-060906-18

Pivčević, S., Kuliš, Z., & Šerić, N. (2016). The pull factors of tourism demand: A panel data analysis for Latin American and Caribbean countries. In *Proceedings of 23rd International Congress Tourism and Hospitality Industry* (pp. 319–333). University of Rijcka, Faculty of Tourism and Hospitality Management.

Plovput d.o.o. Split – arhiva sigurnosti plovidbe.

Pomfret, G., & Bramwell, B. (2016). The characteristics and motivational decisions of outdoor adventure tourists: A review and analysis. *Current Issues in Tourism, 19*(14), 1447–1478.

Pride, W. M., & Ferrell, O. C. (2000). *Marketing: Concepts and strategies*. Houghton Mifflin Co.

Prideaux, B. (2009). *Resort destinations: Evolution, management and development*. Elsevier.

Prideaux, B., Thompson, M., & Pabel, A. (2020). Lessons from Covid-19 can prepare global tourism for the economic transformation needed to combat climate change. *Tourism Geographies, 22*(3), 667–678.

Prorok, V., Šerić, N., & Peronja, I. (2019). Analysis of overall and pure technical efficiency of tourism in Europe. *Transactions on Maritime Science Journal, 8*(2), 219–229.

Ramsdell, G. (2002). The real business of B2B. *McKinsey Quarterly, 3/2002*, 174–184.

Ramsey, T. Z. (Ed.). (2014). *Selected readings in consumer neuroscience & neuromarketing* (2nd ed.). Neurons Inc.

Rašetina, S. (2010). *Fenomen tamnog turizma u kontekstu razvoja selektivnih oblika turizma*. Ekonomski fakultet.

Richards, G. (2019). Culture and tourism: Natural partners or reluctant bedfellows? A perspective paper. *Tourism Review, 75*(1), 232–234.

Ries, A., & Trout, J. (2001). *Positioning: The battle for your mind* (2nd ed.). McGraw-Hill Professional Publishing.

Ringer, G. (2013). *Destinations: Cultural landscapes of tourism*. Routledge.

Ritchie, J. R. B., & Crouch, G. I. (2003). *The competitive destination: A sustainable tourism perspective*. CABI.

Rocco, S., & Hodak, M. (2013). Innovation by design: Bringing design into the focus of SMEs. In *Proceedings e-book, 23rd CROMAR Congress Marketing in a*

Dynamic Environment – Practical and Academic Insights, Lovran, October 24–26, 2013 (pp. 521–536).

Rocco, S., & Pisnik, A. (2014). Developing a conceptual model of relationship between market orientation and design orientation. In *5th EMAC Regional Conference, Book of Proceedings*, Poland, September, 2014 (pp. 177–184).

Ruhanen, L., Moyle, C. I., & Moyle, B. (2019). New directions in sustainable tourism research. *Tourism Review*, *74*(2), 138–149.

Schiffman, L. G., Kanuk, L., & Hansen, H. (2012). *Consumer behaviour: A European outlook*. Harlow.

Seaton, A., & Lennon, J. (2004). *Thanatourism in the early 21st century: Moral panics, ulterior motives and alterior desires*. CABI Publishing.

Seow, D., & Brown, L. (2018). The solo female Asian tourist. *Current Issues in Tourism*, *21*(10), 1187–1206.

Šerić, N. (2003). Importance of remodeling of marketing strategies for the market in the countries in transition. In *Proceedings of 5th International Conference Enterprise in Transition*, Split (pp. 1687–1695).

Šerić, N. (2004). *Kamena svjetla*. Marjan tisak.

Šerić, N. (2008). Realizacija II Faze složenog investicijskog projekta Kamena Svjetla – sanacija i revitalizacija svjetioničarskih zgrada bez ljudske posade. *Gospodarstvo i Okoliš*, *3/90*(XVI), 3–9.

Šerić, N. (2009a). *Razvoj i dizajn proizvoda i upravljanje markom*. Sveučilište u Splitu, Ekonomski fakultet.

Šerić, N. (2009b). *Tržišno poslovanje malog poduzeća*. Sveučilište u Splitu, Ekonomski fakultet.

Šerić, N. (2011). Management of the national touristic brand: The role of the branding strategy in Croatia. *The International Journal of Management Cases*, (Special Issue), 6–11. Access Press Darwen Lancashire.

Šerić, N. (2012a). Brendiranje otoka istočnog Jadrana u funkciji jačanja identiteta turističke destinacije. In *Identitet jadranskog prostora Hrvatske: Retrospekt i prospekt* (pp. 291–307). Ekonomski fakultet.

Šerić, N. (2012b). Brendiranje turističke destinacije temeljeno na identitetu. In *Proceedings of the RT-SEE-2012 Tourism Human Resources Development*, Sarajevo (pp. 428–436).

Šerić, N. (2014). Branding strategy for specialized tourism product. *Advances in management*, *7*(1), 8–12.

Šerić, N. (2016). *Upravljanje proizvodom*. Redak.

Šerić, N. (2017). Lucije Ertorije Kast – iskoristiva platforma kreiranja vrijedne destinacijske ikone Podstrane. *Podstranska revija*, *XVI*(34), 10–13.

Šerić, N. (2018). *Marketing društvenog poduzetništva*. Redak.

Šerić, N. (2019a). Neuromarketing and perception of the touristic destination. In *Proceedings of 3rd International Conference Security of Historical Cities 2019 – panel*.

Šerić, N. (2019b). Inovativan kružni koncept upravljanja dualnom destinacijskom ikonom Podstrane: Od legende Kralja Arthura do povijesne ličnosti Artoriusa Luciusa Kasta. *Podstranska revija*, *XVIII*(37), 10–12.

Šerić, N. (2020). Nacionalni identitet i razvoj specijalizirane turističke ponude. In *XX Paneuropean shipping Conference Split – panel*.

Šerić, N., & Batalić, M. (2018). Marketinško upravljanje informacijama u funkciji jačanja privlačnosti turističke destinacije. *Podstranska revija*, *XVII*(36), 12–15.

Šerić, N., Dadić, M., & Radas, A. (2020). *Logistika hotelskog poduzeća*. Redak.

Šerić, N., Ikač, M., & Vidović, Z. (2002). Disposal of waste water in ecologically sensitive environment of lighthouse. In *Conference Proceedings 44th International Symposium ELMAR*, Zadar (pp. 135–139).

Šerić, N., Jerković, M., & Bučić, K. (2017). Mogućnosti kreiranja turističke marke zaobalne destinacije Svilaja Moseć. In *Zbornik radova Župa Ogorje-Putovima života i vjere između Svilaje i Moseća* (pp. 467–486). Odsjek za povijest Filozofskog fakulteta Sveučilišta u Splitu.

Šerić, N., & Jurišić, M. (2014). *Istraživanje tržišta za turističke subjekte*. Redak.

Šerić, N., & Jurišić, M. (2015). Methodological approach and model analysis for identification of tourist trends. *Journal of Economics and Business, 10*(2015), 47–54.

Šerić, N., Jurišić, M., & Petričević, D. (2015). Neuromarketing potential for tourist destination brand positioning. In *Proceedings of ToSee 3rd International Scientific Conference Tourism in Southern and Eastern Europe 2015*, Opatija (pp. 429–439).

Šerić, N., Kalinić, S., & Žilić, I. (2011). The testing of strategic model of positioning of a new product from the country in transition on the global market. In *Proceedings of the 2011. Researching Economic Development and Entrepreneurship in Transition Economies* (pp. 322–327).

Šerić, N., & Ljubica, J. (2018). *Market research methods in the sport industry*. Emerald Publishing Limited.

Šerić, N., Ljubica, J., & Jerković, M. (2015). Evaluation of the tourist resort strategic management model in the eastern Adriatic litoral. In *Proceedings of the 11. International Conference Challenge of Europe*, Hvar, Croatia (pp. 273–290).

Šerić, N., & Luetić, A. (2016). *Suvremena logistika*. Redak.

Šerić, N., & Luković, T. (2007). Primjena BPD modela razvoja tržišne strategije tranzicijskih tržišta. *Ekonomska Misao i Praksa, 1/2007*, 99–109.

Šerić, N., & Luković, T. (2010). Marketing and environment management for tourism: Croatian experiences. *Academica turistica Tourism & Innovation Journal year, 3*(1–2/2010), 73–80.

Šerić, N., & Luković, T. (2013). *Plan razvoja novih turističkih proizvoda Rivijere Gradac, scientific research*. Ekonomski fakultet Split 2013.

Šerić, N., & Marušić, F. (2019). Tourism promotion of destination for Swedish Emissive market. *Advances in economics and business, 7*(1), 1–8.

Šerić, N., Jakšić Stojanović, A., Jurišić, M., Melović, M., & Marušić, F. (2023). *Marketinške strategije u turizmu i ugostiteljstvu*. Redak Split.

Šerić, N., Melović, M., & Jakšić Stojanović, A. (2023). The role of stakeholders in development of agro tourism in post-transition countries. *Management Journal of Contemporary Management Issues, 28*(special issue), 93–106.

Šerić, N., & Meža, P. (2014). Destination branding through the perception of the tourist: Case from Croatia. In *Proceedings of MakeLearn 2014 Human Capital without Borders Knowledge and Learning for Quality of Life* (pp. 77–87). ToKnowPress.

Šerić, N., Mihanović, A., & Tolj, A. (2020). Model for the development of a specialised dark tourism product. *Transactions on Maritime Science Journal, 9*(2), 324–330.

Šerić, N., Pavlinović, S., & Perišić, M. (2011). Determining the receptive capacity of tourist destinations in the context of the environmental sensitivity of the micro-location. In *Social and cultural implications of multiculturalism* (pp. 89–101).

Faculty of Philosophy in Split/Croatian-Canadian Academic Society. https:// hrcak.srce.hr/en/79139

Šerić, N., & Perišić, M. (2012). *Branding strategy for specialist tourism products in cruise tourism and society: A socio-economic perspective* (pp. 39–46). Springer Verlag.

Šerić, N., Peronja, I., & Marušić, F. (2020). *Upravljanje razvojem specijaliziranog turističkog proizvoda.* Redak.

Šerić, N., Rozga, A., & Luetić, A. (2014). Relationship between business intelligence and supply chain management for marketing decisions. *Universal Journal of Industrial and Business Management, 2*(2), 31–35.

Šerić, N., & Talijančić, J. (2011). Identity of national heritage in function of specialised tourist offer of Croatia. *Journal of Economic Science: Alexandru Ioan Cuza, University Press University of Iasi,* 327–338.

Šerić, N., & Uglešić, D. (2014). The marketing strategies for market niches during recession. In *III Researching Economic Development and Entrepreneurship in Transition Economies Conference Proceedings,* Banja Luka (pp. 327–335).

Šerić, N., Vitner Marković, S., & Petričević, D. (2012). The proposition of the model for managing tourist resources of the border areas – The basis for creating a tourist brand. In *Proceedings of the 2012. Researching Economic Development and Entrepreneurship in Transition Economies,* Banja Luka (pp. 783–790).

Šerić, N., Vitner Marković, S., & Rakušić Cvrtak, K. (2017). *Brendiranje za poduzetnike.* Redak.

Sharpley, R., & Stone, P. R. (2009). *The darker side of travel: The theory and practice of dark tourism.* Channel View Publications.

Sheehan, L., Bornhorst, T., & Brent Ritchie, J. R. (2010). Determinants of tourism success for DMOs & destinations: An empirical examination of stakeholders' perspectives. https://www.sciencedirect.com/science/article/abs/pii/S0261517709001162

Sheth, J. N., Eshghi, A., & Krishnan, B. C. (2001). *Internet marketing.* Harcourt College Publishers Fort Worth.

Sigala, M. (2004). Using data envelopment analysis for measuring and benchmarking productivity in the hotel sector. *Journal of Travel & Tourism Marketing, 16*(2), 39–60.

Šimundić, B., Kuliš, Z., & Šerić, N. (2016). Tourism and economic growth: Evidence for Latin American and Caribbean countries. In *Proceedings of the 23rd International Congress Tourism and Hospitality Industry* (pp. 457–469). University of Rijeka, Faculty of Tourism & Hospitality Management.

Solo Female Travelers. (2022). *Solo female travel trends & statistics.* https:// www.solofemaletravelers.club/solo-female-travel-stats/

Solow, R. M. (2008). The economics of resources or the resources of economics. *Journal of Natural Resources Policy Research, 1,* 69–82.

Soysal-Kurt, H. (2017). Measuring tourism efficiency of European countries by using data envelopment analysis. *European Scientific Journal, 13*(10).

Stainton, H. (2023). What is special interest tourism and why is it so popular? https:// tourismteacher.com/special-interest-tourism/

Stone, P. R. (2006). A dark tourism spectrum: Towards a typology of death and macabre related tourist sites, attractions and exhibitions. *International Interdisciplinary Journal, 54*(2), 145–160. http://hrcak.srce.hr/161464

Stone, P. R. (2013). Dark tourism, heterotopias and post-apocalyptic places – The case of Chernobyl. In L. White & E. Frew (Eds.), *Dark tourism and place identity.* Routledge.

Swarbrooke, J., & Horner, S. (2007). *Consumer behaviour in tourism.* Butterworth Heinemann.

Tarlow, P. (2005). *Dark tourism: The appealing 'dark side' of tourism and more.* Butterworth-Heinemann.

Toma, E. (2014). Regional scale efficiency evaluation by input-oriented data envelopment analysis of tourism sector. *International Journal of Academic Research in Environment and Geography, 1*(1), 15–20.

Tomic, S., & Marcikic Horvat, A. (2016). Evaluation of efficiency in tourism industry. https://www.researchgate.net/publication/332268600_EVALUATION_OF_EFFICIENCY_IN_TOURISM_INDUSTRY

Tran, N. L., & Rudolf, W. (2022). Social media and destination branding in tourism: A systematic review of the literature. *Sustainability, 14*(20), 13528.

Tschapka, M. K. (2006). *Involvement, motivations and setting preference of participants in the adventure tourism activity of scuba diving.* University of Canberra.

Tsung Hung, L. (2013). Influence analysis of community resident support for sustainable tourism development. *Tourism Management, 34*(February), 37–46.

UN. (2020). *Ending poverty.* https://www.un.org/en/sections/issues-depth/poverty-0/index.html

Unearth Women. (2023). *These are the top women's travel trends this year.* https://www.unearthwomen.com/these-are-the-top-womens-travel-trends-this-year/

UNWTO. (2020). *World tourism barometer May 2020, Special focus on the impact of Covid-19.* https://webunwto.s3.eu-west-1.amazonaws.com/s3fs-public/2020-05/Barometer%20-%20May%202020%20-%20Short.pdf

Uysal, M., & Jurowski, C. (1994). Testing the push and pull factors. *Annals of Tourism Research, 21*(4), 844–846.

Vargas-Sanchez, A., Porras-Bueno, N., & Plaza-Mejia, M. (2011). Explaining residents attitudes to tourism – Is universal model possible? *Annals of Tourism Research, 38*(2), 460–480.

Volkman, M. (2022). *How has social media changed the tourism industry?* https://www.solimarinternational.com/how-has-social-media-changed-the-tourism-industry/

Wang, H., & Yan, J. (2022). Effects of social media tourism information quality on destination travel intention: Mediation effect of self-congruity and trust. *Frontiers in Psychology, 13*, 1049149.

Wang, Y. A. (2008). Collaborative destination marketing: Understanding the dynamic process. *Journal of Travel Research, 47*(2), 151–166.

Weaver, D. B. (2006). *Sustainable tourism: Theory and practice.* Routledge.

Wen, J., Kozak, M., Yang, S., & Liu, F. (2021). *Covid-19: Potential effects on Chinese citizens lifestyle and travel.* https://doi.org/10.1108/TR-03-2020-0110

Williams, B. (2023). *40+ female travel statistics (2023!).* https://www.dreambigtravelfarblog.com/blog/female-travel-statistics

WTTC. (2020). *To recovery/beyond: The future of travel & tourism in the wake of Covid-19.* https://wttc.org/Research/To-Recovery-Beyond/moduleId/

Yeap, J. A., Ignatius, J., & Ramayah, T. (2014). Determining consumers' most preferred eWOM platform for movie reviews: A fuzzy analytic hierarchy process approach. *Computers in Human Behavior, 31*, 250–258.

Zhang, H., Song, H., Wen, L., & Liu, C. (2021). *Forecasting tourism recovery amid Covid-19.* https://doi.org/10.1016/j.annals.2

Printed in the USA
CPSIA information can be obtained
at www.ICGtesting.com
JSHW011434200624
65131JS00003B/15